LUMINOUS DAYS

A life-transforming devotional that is surely to illuminate your journey.

Claribel Ramirez

LUMINOUS
Books

Luminous Books
Florida

Typeset by: Michelle Cline

CONTENTS

DEDICATION

This Devotional is dedicated foremost to my best friend the Holy Spirit, to whom I want to be obedient the rest of my life.

To my maternal grandparents who were a great inspiration in my life, "Mama Bellota " and "Papa Fello" I can still remember them, praying daily, many grandchildren were there at that holy hour.

To my mother who unknowingly impacted my life with an open Bible in Psalm 91 on the night table, which I had to learn by heart to ward off evil from my spiritual attacks since I was a child. Just as I will never forget and I am grateful to her sister Aurora for looking out for me specially in prayers. Above all to my closest paternal family who welcomed me and gave me a good upbringing here in the US, they know well who they are, I love them eternally with all my heart. Thanks to my children and my loving husband for their patience and for believing in my visions and dreams. Thanks to Denise Archer for helping me with the English translation of this book.

I cannot forget a very special person in my life, my brother Kevin, whom God used one day to get me out of the spiritual prison in which I was living in without knowing it. These were the words he used; "Sis! the day that you want something, or someone to change in your life, ask God to change you first" these words still resonate in the depths of my being, and just as he suggested it to me I did. Today I recognize that day was inspired by the Holy Spirit, and so my journey began in the search that God would change my life.

And He did and continues to do so, I am a work in progress, I know that God is not done with me yet, I have confidence that He that started the good work will carry it to completion. Thanks be to God!

INTRODUCTION

This devotional is an updated version from my Spanish book published in 2020. Every page will illuminate your life and provide a divine sense of direction. May you be transformed by the presence of the Holy Spirit. At the beginning of each day you shall find a scripture with a powerful name of God that can be used when praying. You will find a reflection for each day along with a prayer and action steps. I know it will provide you with encouragement, inner healing and deliverance from many bondages. Be in expectation of daily blessings with every reading.

God is real, He is omnipresent and is now at the door of your heart knocking and waiting for you to open it, answer His call! God is yearning for you to have an intimate relationship with Him.

Live a purposeful life! This devotional was inspired to edify, strengthen, and direct your path through your journey with the word of God. I ask the Lord to open your spiritual eyes and ears so that you can see and hear him all the time.

As I'm writing these words, the Lord instills in my heart Psalm 46:10 "Be still and know that I am God." Constantly we worry about unnecessary things and we forget the necessity of recognizing Him in all we do beforehand.

Make the decision to advance day by day, guided by the word of God and dedicate the adequate time to meditate in Spirit and in Truth. Remember to intercede for the peace of Israel and of the whole world.

Receive peace that surpasses all understanding now in the Mighty name of Jesus, Never forget that the ultimate price paid for our freedom was Jesus's precious Blood.

Amen!

Although God is infinitely far beyond our ability to understand Him, we will learn that He is the fullness of everything in everything; through the Scriptures He reveals important and specific truths about himself, which will help us to understand him and discover what He is like and thus be drawn to his presence and come to worship him as our only Savior. To get to know Him it is extremely essential to focus every day on Him, on His incomparable love and on His sacrifice for us so that we can have a more intimate relationship with Him.

GOD OUR LORD, HOW GREAT IS YOUR NAME I ALL THE EARTH! ACCORDING TO YOUR NAME, GOD, THIS IS YOUR LOVE TO THE ENDS OF THE EARTH GOD IS KNOWN IN JUDAH; IN ISRAEL HIS NAME IS A HIGH TOWER STRONG IS THE NAME OF GOD; TO HIM SHALL RUN THE RIGHTEOUS AND SHALL BE LIFTED UP.

Ps. 8:1 ~ Ps. 48:10 ~ Ps. 76:1

ADONAI

The Lord, My great Lord.

Yours, O Lord, is the greatness and the power and the glory and the victory and the majesty, indeed everything that is in the heavens and on the earth; Yours is the dominion and kingdom, O Lord, and You exalt Yourself as head overall.

1 Chronicles 29:11 (AMP)

THE POWER OF FAITH

Now faith is the assurance (title deed, confirmation) of things hoped for (divinely guaranteed), and the evidence of things not seen [the conviction of their reality—faith comprehends as fact what cannot be experienced by the physical senses].

Hebrews 11:1 (AMP)

REFLECTION:

Today, let's embrace the power of faith. Faith is the foundation of our relationship with God, the assurance of things hoped for, and the evidence of things not seen. Faith is Believing that nothing is impossible for God when He is on our side. Know that God works His miracles through you and I.

In a world filled with uncertainty and doubt, it's easy to get caught up in others' opinions and perspectives. But as believers, we have a greater truth to hold onto the Word of God, His spoken voice, which is revealed to us as we continuously read the bible, meditate on it and live our lives by it. For example, in *Jn 14:6* Jesus *said to him, I am the way, and the truth, and the life; no one comes to the Father except through me.* There is no other road that you and I can find our way in, through or out of life without having to go through Christ our savior.

He is the solid ground on which we stand, the hope that anchors our souls. When we believe in Him, His promises become a yes and amen, a reality in our lives. Faith is not about seeing to believe, but believing first to then see. It's trusting in God's sovereignty, even when we can't see the outcome right away.

Without Faith it is impossible to please God Moreover without faith we become hopeless and our joy is not complete. My desire is that today you can comprehend that Faith is a primary ingredient for our walk on this earth. You and I can become the bearer of God's voice which is our command and duty.

You and I don't really need a huge amount of believing faith to see those problems we are facing resolve. All we need is to believe without doubt that God can accomplish them through us and in us. *Truly I tell you, if you have faith as small as a mustard seed, you can say to this mountain, 'Move from here to there,' and it will move. Nothing will be impossible for you. Mat 17;20*

I hope this reflection fills your personal backpack with lively tools that would inspire you to share the knowledge God has given you with others, that might be struggling with their belief's system.

LET'S PRAY TOGETHER:

Lord Almighty, help my unbelief and increase my faith today, that I may recognize that it is not necessary to have great faith to obtain supernatural miracles. Heavenly Father, open my spiritual eyes to see beyond what is natural, that I may believe in your benevolence and love for me. Lord, In you there is no variation, you change not, help me understand my authority in you. God of glory, all this I ask in the powerful name of Jesus.

GOD ADONAI may it be done on earth as it is in heaven, Lord of Lords teach me to believe and see in the unseen realm. That I may know that I know that if God is with me, no one can be against me. *Yours, O Lord, is the greatness and the power and the glory and the victory and the majesty.* Amen!

ACTION STEP:

Write down your goals and desires, and next to each one, write a scripture that confirms God's promise.

Read and Meditate on those promises daily.

Sample, believing in mustard seed size faith; If I am dealing with a disease of any kind. I go through the scriptures and find that I'm told in *Isaiah 53:5 He was beaten so we could be whole. He was whipped so we could be healed.* So, every day I will decree and declare myself believing with no doubt that I have been healed. Yes, the pain might persist but I will resist. Persevering, decree that I have been healed by Jesus's stripes. Just hold on to that belief and trust. *God is watchful over His words to perform it. Jer 1:12*

Join a group that studies the scripture so that in that sense you can have accountability. Share your faith forward.

EL-GIBHOR

"THE MIGHTY GOD"

*A remnant will return, a remnant
of Jacob, to the mighty God.*

Isaiah 10:21 (AMP)

GUIDANCE & DIRECTION

*Let me know Your ways, O Lord. Teach me Your paths.
Guide me in Your truth and teach me. For You are the
God of my salvation; For You [and only You] I wait
[expectantly] all day long.*

Psalms 25: 4-5 (AMP)

REFLECTION:

This psalm has been a source of comfort and guidance during difficult times. I remember being taught its existence by an acquaintance named Mary during a challenging moment in my life as a single mom. I was struggling to make ends meet, working multiple jobs, and feeling overwhelmed by the responsibilities of raising two young children alone. Mary shared this psalm with me, and it became a beacon of hope in the darkness.

Since 2009 I have been reciting it daily till this day along with other scriptures I already prayed, Psalm 91 and the Our Father in Matt 6.

I have held on tight to its promise, I've learned to ask for direction and clarity from the Holy Spirit daily, waiting expectantly for His guidance. He is the one who guides me through the ups and downs of life, and I can trust in His sovereignty and His loving-kindness. I learned that every day brings its own lessons as it says in Mat *6:34 So do not worry about tomorrow; for tomorrow will worry about itself. Each day has enough trouble of its own.*

I have experienced His guidance in many ways, from small moments of clarity to significant life-changing events. I have learned to listen to His still, small voice, to seek His counsel in Scripture, and to trust in His promises. This psalm has become a reminder of God's faithfulness and love, a reminder that He is always with me, directing my paths into a good future.

Personal testimony; "I was moved to pray with my daughter Ashley around 2016 or so for 40 days and 40 nights, alternating days where she led the prayer than I did. We didn't prepare anything, just prayed and asked the Holy Spirit to guide us. Despite some frustrating days for me, when she didn't want to perform. But God never failed us. Ashley received many revelations, visions, and scriptures throughout our journey, one day we will write about it. One night, she saw a vision of the Passover *Exo 12:13,14* which she had no prior knowledge of the entirety of the story during that specific time.

This experience showed me God's desire for an intimate relation-ship with our children as well as for us personally. I encourage you to have an open heart and mind, seeking God's guidance and documenting your journey. Just as Ashley and I overcame trials and obstacles through God's precious Blood, you too can become an overcomer."

Stop and read the entirety of the psalm, meditating on its words. Decide to read it for a set number of days, allowing the Holy Spirit to guide you. I assure you it will be a blessing, just as it has been for my family and I. May God's presence direct your paths, and may you find comfort and peace in Him.

LET'S PRAY TOGETHER;
Father, Son and Holy Spirit I ask you at this very moment through the blood of your beloved Son Jesus, cleanse me and open my spiritual eyes and ears so that I can see you and hear your voice guiding me through your green pastures.

Teach me that I can walk towards the destiny that you have pre-pared for me. Wash me white as snow, place people on my path that are willing and open to helping each other in this journey called life. This I ask in the name of Jesus, Amen.

ACTION STEP:

Commit to reading all or some verses of Psalms *25* Or any other scripture the Spirit guides you too, for a set number of days (e.g., 7, 21, or 40) and journal about your experiences and insights.

I invite you to travel the paths that God has laid out for your future. There is power in the word of God. Power in *"THE STRONG GOD"* **EL -GIBHOR**.

Get accustomed to applying the Blood of the Lamb spiritually over your home and your loved ones every single day for divine protection.

Exo 12:13,14 The blood will be a sign for you on the houses where you are, and when I see the blood, I will pass over you. No destructive plague will touch you when I strike Egypt. This is a day you are to commemorate; for the generations to come you shall celebrate it as a festival to the LORD—a lasting ordinance

LUMINOUS DAY 3

EL YISRAEL

The God of Israel

*You, God, are awesome in your sanctuary;
the God of Israel gives power and
strength to his people. Praise be to God!*

Psalms 68:35 (NIV)

VICTORY THROUGH CHRIST

But thanks be to God, who gives us the victory [as conquerors] through our Lord Jesus Christ!

1 Corinthians 15:57 (AMP)

REFLECTION:

Victory is ours through Christ!

Yet, unfortunately we often forget about it. Yes, we will face struggles, but God uses them for our spiritual growth, making us stronger and wiser. He knows our needs before we ask *Matt 6:8* and He is always with us, even in the toughest circumstances. With God we are more than conquerors *Rom 8:37* We can trust that He's working everything out for our good.

Job's story inspires us to trust God despite adversity *Job 2:10*. Let's choose gratitude and thanksgiving, versus fears and doubts, may we not focus on the evil days ahead. His victory on the cross is our victory, and with Him we can overcome anything. We are not alone, and we're not defeated, Jesus is our strength. Let's walk with Him and begin living a life of praise.

I'm reminded of these verses in: *2 Cor 4;8,9 We are hard pressed on every side, but not crushed; perplexed, but not in despair; persecuted, but not abandoned; struck down, but not destroyed.* The struggles and challenges we face today bring us adequate spiritual growth for an unknown tomorrow.

I'm not sure if you know that there are no big problems that take God by surprise. He has already seen the beginning and the end of our lives, the in and outside of all the wagons of our train's journey. He knows the result of every situation you might encounter before it even happens. He knows your needs before you ask Him *Matt 6:8.*

We must consciously and constantly be aware that we are a new creation when we accept Christ as our Lord and savior. He then becomes one with our spirit and dwells on the inside of us. He has already conquered death once and for all. *Rom 6:9,10* Victory belongs to you and I and our generations to come

Be released from the prison of complacency and ingratitude, don't go in hiding mode, your life is not a secret to the father. Learn to live a rewarding life because JESUS defeated death to give you life and life abundantly.

Encounter the love of the father while He is running to embrace you with His open arms of mercy. Praise His Holy name EL **YISRAEL,** worship the God of Israel.

LET'S PRAY TOGETHER:
God, at this very moment I want to release all grievances so that I may live a life in gratitude to your sovereignty, knowing that your victory and presence is with me wherever I go.

Teach me, Holy Spirit, to never stop being thankful regardless of the obstacles and challenges I face.

Lord, deliver me from any and all fears and doubts that might be lingering in my life. Your word says that you have redeemed me from the curse of the law *Gal 3;13*. I declare right now that I am free and your word also tells me that whoever the son sets free is free indeed *Jn 8;36*. Freedom is my portion. I pray in the mighty name of Jesus. Amen!

ACTION STEP:
Write down a hardship situation where you need to declare the power of the blood of Jesus over it and realize you have achieved victory through the shedding of His blood. Ask God to reveal His presence and guidance in that situation.

Be encouraged *Rom 8:37 Yet in all these things we are more than conquerors and gain an overwhelming victory through Him Who loved us.*

Attend church if you don't already, become part of their bible study group, find a prayer group with like-minded people and join them.

Commit some of your time to serve the church and your community. As you plant a seed of kindness and give, so you will get back a harvest at its rightful time.

LUMINOUS DAY 4

ALPHA & OMEGA

"First and Last" "Beginning and End."

And He who sits on the throne said, "Behold, I am making all things new." Also, He said, "Write, for these words are faithful and true [they are accurate, incorruptible, and trustworthy]."

Revelation 21:5-6 (AMP)

PERSISTENT PRAYER AND THANKSGIVING

Be persistent and devoted to prayer, being alert and focused in your prayer life with an attitude of thanksgiving.

Colossians 4:2 (AMP)

REFLECTION:

Prayer is often viewed as a last-minute resource for most, but God urges us to be persistent and devoted to prayer at all times, with an attitude of thanksgiving. This lifestyle in Christ strengthens our relationship with Him and allows us to trust in His provision and guidance when most needed.

God's faithfulness makes us more than conquerors. Let's continually thank Him and praise His name like David often did, *Not to us, O Lord, not to us, But to Your name give glory. Because of Your lovingkindness, because of Your truth and faithfulness. Psalm 115:1* We can learn to thank Jesus for the desires of our hearts, before we get them into our hands, if you believe you will get it even if it arrives at the 11th hour, He is our provider.

"The book of Ephesians is a powerful tool for unlocking spiritual growth, if you ever need a master key to open a rustic door knob the book of Ephesians is one of those master keys available for you and I. *Eph 6:18 And pray in the Spirit on all occasions with all kinds of prayers and requests. With this in mind, be alert and always keep on praying for all the Lord's people.* It's a reminder to pray in our heavenly languish and with persistence interceding for all God's people.

This consistent prayer relationship with God empowers us to accomplish anything and guarantees peace amidst troubles. As Jesus promises in Jn 16:33 We can have *perfect peace in Him,* despite worldly tribulations. Our trust must be placed in the One who called us, knowing He strengthens us to face life's storms.

Let's stay firm in our faith, unsinkable in the midst of challenges." **God is THE ALPHA AND THE OMEGA**, our present help in times of trouble.

LET'S PRAY TOGETHER:

Father God, today with the great love you have for me, teach me to be willing to pray at all times. That I may intercede for the weakest and neediest of your sheep flock.

Give me wisdom to understand the need to have an intimate relationship with your Holy Spirit and at the same time grant me the knowledge of a close communion with your beloved Son. Place in my heart the desire to seek you day and night in the name of Jesus. Amen!

ACTION STEP:

Spend at least 5–10 minutes praying every day for God's sheep, interceding for their needs and struggles. Don't stop praying!!

Ask God to strengthen your prayer life and guide you to encounter the right people to pray for them.

Remember you and I are victors not victims, Jesus won the victory over 2000 years ago to bring us freedom and unity in Him.

Set time apart to meet with the Lord, obedience creates miracles.

LUMINOUS DAY 5

GOD SABAOTH

" Lord of Host, The Lord of the armies"

*This man went up from his city each year to worship
and sacrifice to the Lord of hosts at Shiloh.
Hophni and Phinehas, the two sons of Eli,
were priests to the Lord there.*

I Samuel 1:3 (AMP)

TRUSTING IN GOD'S TIMING

But as for me, I will look expectantly for the Lord and with confidence in Him I will keep watch; I will wait [with confident expectation] for the God of my salvation. My God will hear me.

Micah 7:7 (AMP)

REFLECTION:

As I reflect on this verse, I am reminded of the importance of waiting on the Lord's timing. It's easy to get impatient and to try to take control over our current situation, but this verse encourages us to wait expectantly for the Lord, with confidence in His plans.

This means trusting that He has our best interests at heart, even when we can't see the bigger picture. But we aren't without an assignment during the waiting season, we just have to be watchful to see and hear what he tells us to do and so we commit to do it to the best of our ability.

We should not trust in our own ways of thinking patterns or in the ways we look at the things around us. Why not? Because many times we can be totally deceived by those things. It is imperative to have a biblical parameter of the truth, which will prevent us from committing graveyard mistakes that may in a near future bring us catastrophic results literally speaking.

A verse just came to mind. *Luke 6:47-49 I will show you what it's like when someone comes to me, listens to my teaching, and then follows it. 48 It is like a person building a house who digs deep and lays the foundation on solid rock. When the floodwaters rise and break against that house, it stands firm because it is well built. 49 But anyone who hears and doesn't obey is like a person who builds a house right on the ground, without a foundation. When the floods sweep down against that house, it will collapse into a heap of ruins*

In this parable the takeaway is that when you and I seek God, we listen to His commands, what He tells us to do and put it into action right away. With God on our side we will be able to make wise decisions.

The torrential waves of life will not be able to bring us down. Immediate obedience gives us His total support as we stand on solid ground, it will guarantee that when the strong problematic winds arise, we will be able to stand firmly. It is important to be attentive to the still small voice that speaks to us.

Prov 3:5-7 Urges us to *lean on the Lord with all our heart and mind, and not rely on our own understanding*. This can be a challenging concept to put into practice, especially when we feel like we have a good handle on our lives. But the truth is that our wisdom and understanding are limited, and we need God's guidance to navigate life's complexities. By acknowledging Him in all our ways, we can trust that He will direct our paths and lead us to success.

This reminds me of something that happened to me many years ago. Well, the Lord has always given me dreams and visions since I was a young girl, but in those times, I did not know they came from Him.

During this situation I had to make a huge decision whether to leave everything behind in Florida and start over back home in Boston or to continue a path that was literally destroying me. Deep down consciously or unconsciously I knew the right thing to do and that was to move forward and not look back.

I remember that night I prayed to God in this way. Father God, I don't want to look like a failure if I go back but I want to be obedient to you. To shorten the story, that night I had a dream and in it I was preparing my luggage for a flight I had to take. When I woke up and remembered the dream, I immediately knew what I had to do.

Yes, I was heartbroken at the time and it wasn't easy but it had to be done. Looking forward to where I am today, I made the best decision of my life, guided by God.

God speaks in many ways and sometimes He is going to guide you to take rapid actions as if your life depends on it. Always be in expectancy. *This is the confidence we have in approaching God: that if we ask anything according to his will, he hears us. 1 Jn 5:14*

LET'S PRAY TOGETHER:

I declare and prophesy that The Lord of Heaven's Armies is with me and with all my generations guiding us in our journey.

The God of Israel is my strength. The Holy Spirit teaches and guides me in all my steps, I am not alone. God is with me wherever I go, He has not abandoned me, **GOD SABAOTH**, The God of Host and His angel's armies are with us.

He guides me with His victorious right hand. I will not take my eyes of the Lord; you are the God of my salvation. This I pray in the mighty name of Jesus. Amen!

ACTION STEPS:

Be open to hearing God's voice, whether through dreams, prayer, or other means.

Trust that He is speaking to you and guiding you towards His divine plan for your life and take time to seek God's direction in all decisions making.

Reading the scriptures daily will refresh your soul.

King David reminds us; *I lift up my eyes to the mountains, where does my help come from? My help comes from the Lord, the Maker of heaven and earth, He will not let your foot slip, He who watches over you will not slumber indeed, He who watches over Israel will neither slumber nor sleep. Psalms 121:1-4*

SHALOM

"The Lord is our Peace"

Then Gideon built an altar there to the Lord and named it The Lord is Peace. To this day it is still in Ophrah, of the Abiezrites.

Judges 6:24 (AMP)

UNITY AND PEACE IN CHRIST

*For He Himself is our peace and our bond of unity.
He who made both groups— [Jews and Gentiles]—into
one body and broke down the barrier, the dividing wall
[of spiritual antagonism between us],*

Ephesians 2:14 (AMP)

REFLECTION:

SHALOM on this beautiful day that the Lord has made. When we think of the word shalom, we might automatically think of peace, which is correct, but in reality it is deeper than just peace. Let us quickly look at its meaning according to the original language. In the Hebrew word (שָׁלוֹם šālōm;) it means peace, harmony, wholeness, completeness, prosperity, welfare and tranquility at the same time, it can be used idiomatically to mean both hello and goodbye.

The reason I wanted it to bring its meaning up is because after you understand the context behind its roots, it's easier to digest the main verse. In Christ you and I are whole, we are harmoniously bond. We are one in Chris not simply by mere words but by deeds and in spirit.

Jesus died to reconcile us to the father, to redeem us from the curse of the law, to return to us what had been lost in the garden of Eden. He died so you and I could encounter wholeness, completeness and prosperity in its entirety through him.

Think of this: Jesus is our bond. Let's say that you have a picture frame and inside of it your favorite picture of all times, maybe it's of a family member, possibly a person that has passed away like grandparents. One day you come home and that picture frame is broken and so is the picture that was inside, it's been ripped to pieces by your adorable loving pet. Let's say you don't have a copy of it and hypothetically speaking It can only be restored by adding glue or bond to the back of it and so you do it and you save the day.

This brings us back to the main verse, Jesus accomplished far more than a simple bond between us. He accomplished unity for you and I forever and ever. All and any separation from Christ was put aside by His death and resurrection. We are one new man, a new breed, a new creation for His glory. In that newness of life the Lord wants to fill us with His harmonious peace.

Yes, too often Satan will challenge us by using the tactics of our own fears in life. But you and I have many promises to stand on; *But the Advocate, the Holy Spirit, whom the Father will send in my name, will teach you all things and will remind you of everything I have said to you. Peace I leave with you; my peace I give you. I do not give to you as the world gives. Do not let your hearts be troubled and do not be afraid. Jn 14:26–27*

We are not alone here on earth, we have a Holy counselor that wants us to be united in Christ the son, to become one. *And the peace of God, which transcends all understanding, will guard your hearts and your minds in Christ Jesus Phil 4:7*

LET'S PRAY TOGETHER:

Father, embrace me with your Peace, bond me in unity to yourself. Take me to your Most Holy place where I can immerse myself in your Holy presence.

Holy Ghost, teach me to treat everyone with the same love that you show me every day, that I may share your shalom with others. Give me wisdom and understanding, this I ask you in the powerful name of Yeshua Hamashiach. Amen!

ACTION STEPS:

Meditate on His peaceful presence. Ask the Holy Spirit for wisdom and understanding in times of uncertainty, immerse yourself in His love.

During these torrential times we are dealing with a world-wide war zone, political instability and financial inflation. Seek God's guidance.

Read God's word daily, remember these events are temporal, *heaven and earth will pass away but God's words will not pass away;* it will remain. ***SHALOM!***

LUMINOUS DAY 7

ELOHIM CHASEDDI

"The God of Mercy"

The God of my mercy shall prevent me:
God shall let me see my desire upon mine enemies.

Psalm 59:10 KJV

THANKFUL WORSHIPERS

O give thanks to the Lord, for He is good;
For His lovingkindness endures forever.

1 Chronicles 16:34 (AMP)

REFLECTION:

Enter the throne of grace with thanksgiving! I exalt your Holy name; my Lord and my God, Holy of Israel. I thank you for Your everlasting love and mercy, I will forever bless Your Holy name!

Like David, Sing Psalms to the Lord, *Ps 40:3 He put a new song in my mouth, a hymn of praise to our God. Many will see and fear the Lord and put their trust in Him. Ps 146:1-2 Praise the Lord! Praise the Lord, my soul. I will praise the Lord all my life; I will sing praise to my God as long as I live.*

Let us remember God's covenant with our forefathers, of which we are partakers of. Let us thank Him in advance and praise Him for being a good Father, who loves us and desires a personal relationship with us.

These are tumultuous times we are riding on, where our human rights, beliefs and moral values are being challenged, nevertheless we can find peace in God's presence. May we *not conform to this world but rather be transformed t*hrough worshiping the Holy one.

Yes, an evil agenda has risen up against us and our future generations. Strange ideologies are being taught in the schools, wrong is being called right and right is called wrong. We are in unprecedented times, wrongful laws are being implemented and our voices aren't being heard. Our religious freedom is being violated and silenced.

The other day I had a quick vision of the cover of a new book the Lord gave me; I saw a picture of a person looking inside a locked prison cell. What was interesting was that his body was outside the cell but the mind/ brain was locked on the inside. What a terrifying thing to see; and to think that in this day and age there are many people who are feeling imprisoned outside a cell, their minds and bodies are split, even people we love. So many are lost in their own tormenting thoughts and dark pathways.

A high price tag has been paid to accomplish our freedom in order that you and I can walk in wholeness. *Jn 3:16 For God so loved the world that he gave his one and only Son, that whoever believes in him shall not perish but have eternal life.*

Thank you, Jesus! God the Son deserves all the glory and all the honor both in heaven and on earth. Let's not keep our mouths shut, begin worshiping, praising and thanking Him. Glory to the King of Kings! Our Lord and savior.

LET'S PRAY TOGETHER:
Holy Spirit, I thank you for guiding me, I ask you to teach me to have a grateful heart in every situation.

May I put your love and mercy into practice with those around me every day of my life. Open my spiritual eyes so that I can see my neighbor with the love that you have for them. That I may receive grace to forgive those who have hurt me and forget their offenses. I ask this in the Holy name of Jesus. Amen!

ACTION STEPS:
Begin your day with thanksgiving. Take 5 minutes each morning to praise God. Read and meditate on *Psalms 40 and 146,* and let them inspire your own praise and worship.

Reflect on your relationship with God, ask the Holy Spirit to guide you. *Micah 6:8 He has shown you, O mortal, what is good. And what does the LORD require of you? To act justly and to love mercy and to walk humbly with your God.*

LUMINOUS DAY 8

EL SHADDAI

"God Almighty"

But his bow remained firm and steady [in the Strength that does not fail], For his arms were made strong and agile. By the hands of the Mighty One of Jacob, (By the name of the Shepherd, the Stone of Israel), "The blessings of your father Are greater than the blessings of my ancestors [Abraham and Isaac] Up to the utmost bound of the everlasting hills; They shall be on the head of Joseph, even on the crown of the head of him who was the distinguished one and the one who is prince among (separate from) his brothers.

Genesis 49:24-26 (AMP)

INTERCEDING FOR GOD'S PEOPLE

"If anyone sees his brother committing a sin that does not lead to death, he will pray and ask [on the believer's behalf] and God will for him give life to those whose sin is not leading to death. There is a sin that leads to death; I do not say that one should pray for this [kind of sin]."

1 John 5:16 (AMP)

REFLECTION:

As believers, we need to be interceding for one another and not condemning. Let us never forget what God has already accomplished in our own lifetime. We all have a story of how God has freed us from our past. Instead of pointing out others' wrongdoings, let us come together to pray and intercede for their salvation.

We are called to be intercessors, not judges. Stand on the platform of prayer and ask God for strength, grace, and the right perspective to be able to help. *Who are you to judge someone else's servant? To their own master, servants stand or fall. And they will stand, for the Lord is able to make them stand. Rom 14:4*

God almighty makes no distinction of persons we together can bring about the change in people's lives by interceding for them. As believers we are to be the solution wherever we go.

Intercession is a powerful tool that advances the Kingdom of God. When we intercede for someone, the darkness that surrounds them dissipates, and the light of God breaks through, to bring about the transformation they need.

Embrace the power of love through intercession, knowing the enormous potential of miraculous changes it can bring on those around or far apart from us. As we pray for others, we become agents of hope and instruments of God's redemption. Meditate on these truths.

First of all, then, I urge that supplications, prayers, intercessions, and thanksgivings be made for all people, for kings and all who are in high positions, that we may lead a peaceful and quiet life, godly and dignified in every way. 1 Tim 2:1,2

Therefore, confess your sins to one another and pray for one another, that you may be healed. The prayer of a righteous person has great power as it is working. Jm 5:16

LET'S PRAY TOGETHER:

Mighty God full of justice, there is no God like you, I praise your holy name. *Ps 104:31 May the glory of the Lord endure forever; May the Lord rejoice and be glad in His works.*

The glory of the Lord is eternal! I worship you, I will rejoice in the almighty. My Lord and my God, who do you want me to intercede for on this day, week or month?

Renew my mind so that I can see through your eyes and align my thoughts with yours, as they are far above mine. I ask you to give me the knowledge and revelation to be a blessing to others. In the mighty name of Yeshua. Amen!

ACTION STEPS:

Identify who God wants you to intercede for?

My example; Lord, I ask you to send your warring angels to deliver those children and anyone that is being sexually abused. May your angels liberate those that have been kidnapped, help the authorities bring them home safe and take their captors to justice. For those that are part of a gang but want to leave behind that lifestyle, help them be set free.

Ask God to bring someone to mind who needs prayers. Pray for God's light to shine in their life, and for their heart to be transformed by His love, Persevere in prayer. Don't give up on them.

LUMINOUS DAY 9

JEHOVAH-GMOLAH

"The God of Recompense"

*A destroyer will come against Babylon:
her warriors will be captured, and their bows will be broken.
For the Lord is a God of retribution; he will repay in full.*

Jeremiah 51:56 (NIV)

THE TITHE OPENS THE FLOODGATES OF HEAVEN

And all the tithe (tenth part) of the land, whether the seed of the land or the fruit of the tree, is the Lord's; it is holy to the Lord.

Leviticus 27:30 (AMP)

REFLECTION:

Tithing is a topic that many believers avoid discussing, but it's a crucial aspect of our relationship with God. Some argue that tithing is an Old Testament concept, no longer relevant today. Others claim that it's a mandatory 10% payment to the church, without considering the context and purpose of tithing. The following passage reveals that tithing is not just about giving a portion of our income, but about trusting God with our finances and acknowledging His sovereignty over our lives. When we tithe, we're declaring that God is our provider and that we rely on His blessings and guidance.

In Malachi 3:8-10, God confronts the Israelites for robbing Him of the tithes and offerings. He says, "Bring the whole tithe into the storehouse, that there may be food in my house. Test me in this," says the Lord Almighty, "and see if I will not throw open the floodgates of heaven and pour out so much blessing that there will not be room enough to store it."

Some may argue that the church mishandles finances, and therefore, they refuse to tithe. However, this excuse only reveals our lack of trust in God's ability to oversee our gifts. We must remember that our tithes and offerings are not solely for the church's benefit but for the advancement of God's kingdom.

In *Luke 21*, Jesus observes the rich giving their gifts and the poor widow giving her last two coins. He declares that the widow has given more than all the others, for she gave all she had. Her offering was from the heart, she was not concerned whether she was going to have anything to eat or not, she was grateful, I'm sure she had the knowledge of who her provider was. while the rich gave from their abundance, probably measuring how much they had left in their safe place. This story highlights the heart of tithing: it's not simply about the amount we give but the attitude with which we give.

When we tithe with a cheerful and obedient heart, we open ourselves to God's blessings and multiplication. I've experienced this personally, and I've seen God's favor and provision over my life.

Let's not rob God of what belongs to Him. Let's trust Him with our finances and tithe with a heart of gratitude and faith. As we do, we'll experience the floodgates of heaven opening, pouring out blessings that we will not be able to contain.

The Lord gave me this verse over 16 years ago and I have been able to see the greatness of my God on so many levels because I obeyed. *Luke 16:10 "He who is faithful in an extraordinarily little thing is also faithful in much; and he who is dishonest in an extraordinarily little thing is also dishonest in much.* This is one of my living testimonies, on a monthly basis I have been able to share financial support with many people and organizations. Especially an organization called "Save the Children". Ashley and Jeremy chose it when they were very young. Today in 2024 I still contribute.

Today you have an opportunity to be part of our international organization to help children and families in need overseas. GR Eternal Foundation Inc–eternalshift.com Becoming a monthly member will help us reach more families. Thanks in advance for your contributions.

LET'S PRAY PRAYER:
Dear Lord, give me a generous heart, That every time I have to tithe, I can do it from a place of love, you are **EL GMOLAH**; The God of Recompense and retribution.

I want to be a blessing. Guide me to be a faithful steward of your resources. Beloved Jesus, teach me your ways, all this I ask in the mighty name of Jesus. Amen!

ACTION STEPS:

Reflect on your tithing habits. Are you tithing regularly? Are you giving from a place of abundance or poverty?

Pray for guidance*: Ask God to guide you in your financial decisions and show you how to tithe with a cheerful heart.

Find a reputable organization to help, this is aside from tithing, your gifts will be use to advance God's kingdom.

LUMINOUS DAY 10

ELOHIM

"The Living God"

In the beginning God (Elohim) created [by forming from nothing] the heavens and the earth. -God saw that the light was good (pleasing, useful) and He affirmed and sustained it; and God separated the light [distinguishing it] from the darkness.

Genesis 1:1,4 (AMP)

EMBRACE YOUR SEASON

*There is a time for everything, and a season f
or every activity under the heavens:*

*a time to be born and a time to die, a time to plant and a time
to uproot, a time to kill and a time to heal, a time to tear down
and a time to build, a time to weep and a time to laugh, a time
to mourn and a time to dance, a time to scatter stones and a
time to gather them, a time to embrace and a time to refrain
from embracing, a time to search and a time to give up, a time
to keep and a time to throw away, a time to tear and a time to
mend, a time to be silent and a time to speak, a time to love
and a time to hate, a time for war and a time for peace..*

Ecclesiastes 3:1-8

REFLECTION:

In the tapestry of life, God weaves an intricate pattern of sea-
sons, each one a unique opportunity for growth, learning, and
transformation. As I ponder on the wisdom of Ecclesiastes 3 I
am reminded that every moment, every experience, and every
breath is a sacred gift from the Divine.

In this present season, let's invite the Holy Spirit to illuminate our
path, to reveal the hidden treasures of God's plan, and to guide
us in the way of peace. Let's surrender our fears, doubts, and
limitations, trusting that God's grace is sufficient.

Like Queen Esther, you and I recognize that we have been chosen
for such a time as this, to be a light in the darkness, to bring hope
to the hopeless, and to share the love of God with a world in need.
Embrace your true identity as a child of God, beloved, redeemed,
and empowered to fulfill your purpose.

On today's reflection, let yourself be guided by God's presence.
Take a cup of coffee or simply your favorite drink, or let it be on

an empty stomach if you desire. But don't complicate it, find a quiet place and let **ELOHIM** the living God flow to and through you with a fresh revelation. Discern, Is it a time to keep or is it a time to throw away?

It's a new season! Let Jesus illuminate your soul through these verses and teach you that for everything under the sun there is a precise moment.

Recognizing your season now it's extremely important. You and I can join together in this reflection at this moment as the word affirms us in *Matt 18:20 "For where two or three are gathered in my name, there am I among them."* Come, Join us, The Father, the Son and the Holy Spirit. You and I are a majority, let us unite our faith spiritually, intertwine our forces to believe together for your miracle.

As you walk in faith, trust that God's perfect timing will unfold wherever you are. Let's confess the word together, there is no harm but much to be accomplished in this new season. *Romans 10:9 because if you acknowledge and confess with your mouth that Jesus is Lord [recognizing His power, authority, and majesty as God], and believe in your heart that God raised Him from the dead, you will be saved.* Believe it in your heart!

LET'S PRAY TOGETHER:
Good God, in this hour I ask you to open my eyes and spiritual ears, at this very moment. Cleanse me with your precious Blood, I want to be ready for this new season in my journey.

Give me the revelation on what I must do to begin to live the purpose for which you've created me.

Holy Spirit, heal those areas of my heart that are burdened by not seeing my prayers answered when I wanted them, so that I can understand there is a dew season for everything under the sun. Heavenly Father I know that you will supply all of my needs according to your riches and glory. **ELOHIM** I trust in you, I pray and trust in the mighty name of your son Jesus. Amen!

ACTION STEPS:

Reflect on your current season, take time to meditate and ask God to reveal to you where you are in your journey.

Seek to Identify your purpose and knock on the door to receive your spiritual healing. Ask God to give you wisdom and deliverance in any areas you might have fear and doubt.

Embrace your true self, accept who God created you to be, and don't settle for less. Share life and joy with others.

Be a light in the darkness, and share God's love and peace with those around you.

LUMINOUS DAY 11

YAHWEH HESED

"God of Grace"

God decided in advance to adopt us into his own family by bringing us to himself through Jesus Christ. This is what he wanted to do, and it gave him great pleasure. So, we praise God for the glorious grace he has poured out on us who belong to his dear Son. He is so rich in kindness and grace that he purchased our freedom with the blood of his Son and forgave our sins. He has showered his kindness on us, along with all wisdom and understanding.

Ephesians 1:5-8 (NLT)

THE POWER OF ASKING

*If you ask Me anything in My name
[as My representative], I will do it.*

John 14:14 (AMP)

REFLECTION:

Too many of us miss out on God's miracles because we complicate the simplicity of His promises. But what if we could approach Him with childlike faith and receive the revelation of His power? Let's dive into the truth of John 14:14 and unlock the secrets of asking in Jesus' name.

In the majestic name of Jesus, we have the power to move mountains and uproot the impossible. But do we truly understand the simplicity of it all? As we delve into the mystery of the Trinity, we discover that God the Father, Son, and Holy Spirit are one in purpose and unity. I feel led to go a little deeper into this topic.

A perfect union! The father tells us in *Genesis 1: 1* that He created heaven and earth which makes Him our creator. Of the son we are told in *John 4:42* that He is truly the Savior of the world, so Jesus is our Savior. And the Holy Spirit in *John 16:13* is revealed to us as the Spirit of Truth, our ultimate source of truth. By this tremendous revelation we must understand how it is that they become one person, again God the Trinity.

Remember that Jesus said in *Jn 14:10 Do you not believe that I am in the Father, and the Father is in Me? The words I say to you I do not say on My own initiative or authority, but the Father, abiding continually in Me, does His works [His attesting miracles and acts of power].* Let's complete the Holy Trinity. *Luke 4:1 Now Jesus, full of [and in perfect communication with] the Holy Spirit, returned from Jordan and was led by the Spirit in the wilderness.* The divinity, three in one, and so are you and me one with God.

Like the fig tree that withered at Jesus' command, our lives can be transformed by the power of His name. But we must approach Him with faith and humility, recognizing that our prayers are not mere requests but declarations of His sovereignty and mercy.

As we stand on the promises of *Dt 7:14* and *Ps 2:8,* we are assured that our prayers are not in vain. God desires to bless us above all peoples, to make us fruitful and prosperous in all we do. His grace is our unmerited favor, His love our guiding light. God is always looking for people to speak His words for Him to perform it and manifest. He said this in *Jer 1:12 The LORD said to me, You have seen correctly, for I am watching to see that my word is fulfilled.*

I encourage you, through the love, grace, and fellowship of the Holy Spirit, to believe in the all-powerful name of Jesus. We are told in the book of Mt 28:18 *And Jesus came and spoke to them, saying: All authority has been given to Me in heaven and on earth."* We too have this power and authority through Jesus Christ.

LET'S PRAY TOGETHER:
Eternal Father, **YAHWEH HESED**, God of grace, in this moment I ask you to pour your love over my life, that I may feel your closeness wherever I go. Enlighten my mind so that I can understand when I do wrong in your eyes, so that I may change my course and do good.

Holy Spirit teach me to depend solely upon your guidance. That I may know that all difficulties, illnesses and or present financial problems can be solved through you.

I stand in your word; *Ask of Me, and I will assuredly give [You] the nations as Your inheritance, And the ends of the earth as Your possession.' Ps 2:8* Lord, I want to enter your secret place knowing that everything in you is a yes and an amen! Glory to you Lord, Thank you in advance for all your unmerited favors towards me. All this I ask in Jesus's name. Amen!

ACTION STEPS:

Take a moment to pray with Conviction, faith and confidence, asking God specifically for wants and needs in your life. Believe you already got it!

Share Your Testimony: Share a time when God answered your prayer in a miraculous way and encourage others to do the same.

Meditate and Reflect on God's promises, and ask God to reveal His plans and purposes for your life during this season.

Ask for words of knowledge to share with others.

LUMINOUS DAY 12

УАНШЕН
MEKODDISHKEM

"The Lord who sanctifies."

"But as for you, say to the Israelites, 'You shall most certainly observe My Sabbaths, for it is a sign between Me and you throughout your generations, so that you may know [without any doubt] and acknowledge that I am THE LORD who sanctifies you and sets you apart [for Myself].

Exodus 31:13 (AMP)

UNCOVERING HIDDEN BLESSINGS

*Call to Me and I will answer you and tell you
[and even show you] great and mighty things,
[things which have been confined and hidden], which
you do not know and understand and cannot distinguish.'*

Jeremiah 33:3 (AMP)

REFLECTION:

God has hidden treasures that are waiting to be uncovered by you and I. Jeremiah invites us to call upon Him, and He promises to answer and show us great and mighty things. Are you ready to discover these secrets & hidden blessings?

YAHWEH MEKODDISHKEN, God who sanctifies has called you and I by our names, He has prepared for us and our love ones a table to sit at, There is many mansions in the father's house where He has prepared a place for us, we cannot even imagine in our human minds what that could look like.

Let's read the following together; *1 Cor 2:9 However, as it is written: What no eye has seen, what no ear has heard, and what no human mind has conceived" the things God has prepared for those who love him.*

I surely love the Lord, do you? Those inconceivable things are for us and our generations.

In the majestic name of Jesus, we have access to God's kingdom and heavenly places. As we call upon His name and walk in unity with His spirit, He promises to answer and show us greater things. His desire is for us to know Him intimately, to love Him with all our hearts, and to follow His commands.

As we abide in Him, we can experience a full, prosperous, and abundant life, receiving all that He has prepared for us. It tells us in *Prov 10:22 "The blessing of the Lord brings [true] riches, And He adds no sorrow to it [for it comes as a blessing from God]."* As you and I walk in obedience to our loving father, we will find out that He changes not and all His promises for us in Christ Jesus are yes and amen.

LET'S PRAY TOGETHER:

YAHWEH MEKODDISHKEN God who sanctifies me, I ask you today, help me trust and believe in your word. May I hold onto your promises for my life, both physically and spiritually, knowing that what you say you will fulfill.

Father there is no shadow of variation in you. I want to experience a true relationship and communion with you, I want to touch the edge of your garment.

I am no longer satisfied with only sitting in the pew, I desire to serve you and my community wholeheartedly.

Father, provide me with your revelation that you dwell in me. I want to praise your holy name together with your angels. I ask all this in the name of Jesus the Messiah "Yeshua HaMashiach" Amen!

ACTION STEPS:

I urge you to take at least 5 minutes every day to meditate and delight in Holy scriptures. Reflect on how you can apply the principles of Jeremiah 33:3 to your present situation and begin journaling.

Ask God to give you access to receive revelation for your divine purpose. Ask Yourself What are the areas in your life where you need God's guidance and blessings?

Take a moment to call upon Jesus its name, asking Him to reveal His hidden blessing for your life.

LUMINOUS DAY 13

JEHOVAH-SHAMMAH

"Jehovah is there. The lord is my companion."

*The distance around the city shall be
18,000 (4 x 4,500) cubits; and the name of the city
from that day [and ever after] shall be, 'The Lord is There.'"*

Ezekiel 48:35 (AMP)

FORGIVENESS BRINGS FREEDOM

And forgive us our debts, as we have forgiven our debtors [letting go of both the wrong and the resentment].

Matthew 6:12 (AMP)

REFLECTION:

"Forgiveness it's a crucial step towards healing, wholeness and a prosperous soul. Matthew reminds us that forgiveness is not only a virtue but a necessity for our own freedom.

Let's dive into the truth of forgiveness and discover the liberty it brings. In the powerful name of Jesus, we have the power to forgive and be forgiven. The cross is our finishing line, where we can lay down our burdens and receive complete pardon and redemption.

Eph 1:7 Reminds us how enriched is His loving grace, which paid the penalty for our sin. *In Him we have redemption [that is, our deliverance and salvation] through His blood, [which paid the penalty for our sin and resulted in] the forgiveness and complete pardon of our sin, in accordance with the riches of His grace.*

Jesus' final moments on the cross and His last Seven statements on it, also shows us a great significance about forgiving. I'll only mention one expression of love and redemption, culminating in the ultimate act of forgiveness:

Father, forgive them, for they do not know what they are doing. Lk 23:34

In this moment, Jesus exemplifies the true meaning of forgiveness, even in the face of unimaginable pain and betrayal. As we reflect on our own lives, we're reminded that we too have been forgiven, pardoned, and redeemed by His sacrifice. The weight of resentment and bitterness dissipates, replaced by the liberating power of forgiveness.

Will you take this step towards freedom today?

Let us embrace this divine completion and allow it to transform our lives. As we let go of the past, we're restored to wholeness in Christ Jesus. The Father's love and grace await us, ready to set us free from the shackles of resentment.

LET'S PRAY TOGETHER:

Dear, Yahweh; Almighty God, **JEHOVAH-SHAMMAH** The Lord is my companion, you know my going to bed and my awakening, you know if I cry or if I smile, I ask you on this day to heal my wounds.

Holy Spirit, teach me to forgive, I want to be set free from the soul ties and chains that I am dragging with my bitterness.

Wash me with your water and blood that came out of your side on the cross and free my mind, body and soul. I declare: *So if the Son makes you free, you are unquestionably free. John 8:36 Then He said to her, Your sins are forgiven. Luke 7:48* In the mighty name of Jesus. Amen!

ACTION STEPS:

Take a moment to write down the names of those you need to forgive or vice versa and pray for them. Ask God to help you let go of any bitterness and resentment, and receive His peace.

Read and Meditate on *Col 3:13* throughout the day.

Declare and decree you are free every time your thoughts want to remind you of the old offenses.

LUMINOUS DAY 14

YAHWEH GO'EL

"THE REDEEMER"

This is what the Lord your Redeemer, the Holy One of Israel says, "For your sake I have sent [one] to Babylon. And I will bring down all of them as fugitives, Even the Chaldeans [who reign in Babylon], into the ships over which they rejoiced.

Isaiah 43:14 (AMP)

THE POWER OF OBEDIENCE

Then Mary said, "Behold, I am the servant of the Lord; may it be done to me according to your word." And the angel left her.

Luke 1:38 (AMP)

REFLECTION:

Mary's humble response to the angel Gabriel, changed the course of history. Her obedience opened the door for Jesus' arrival, to bring redemption to humanity along with His resurrection power.

Mary's example teaches us the importance of obedience in our journey with God. When we surrender to His will, we then begin experiencing His presence and guidance In our lives. John the Baptist, in the womb of his mother, recognized the Lord's presence in Mary's womb when she arrived to visit Elizabeth, his mom.

Can you only imagine and fathom what this could mean, an unborn baby is able to experience and have knowledge of what is going on in the outside world. John is just another living testimony to the power of obedience.

On the other hand, walking in disobedience leads to a life of turmoil and unrest. *Lk12:47-48 The servant who knows the master's will and does not get ready or does not do what the master wants will be beaten with many blows. 48 But the one who does not know and does things deserving punishment will be beaten with few blows. From everyone who has been given much, much will be demanded; and from the one who has been entrusted with much, much more will be asked.*

What a tremendous warning for us all, that knowing God's will and failing to act on it, can have a negative impact along with spiritual stagnation. *Jm 4:17* Goes as far as to tell us that not doing what we know is right it's considered sin.

Our Redeemer *Is 47:4*, the Lord of hosts, shed His blood for us. Let us surrender to His will, so we could experience the joy and peace in the midst of any storm we may encounter. Take the leap of faith and trust in His guidance. Your life will never be the same.

As you and I heed the call to obeying the Lord, trusting in His goodness. We can find many other examples in the scriptures that urge us to listen and take action to the right path. *Dt 11:28* and *Eph 5:6* are a few verses warning us of the consequences of turning away from God's commands. Jonah is another perfect example, read chapter 1 & 2.

On the other hand, read this amazing and empowering promise we can activate right now; *For I command you today to love the LORD your God, to walk in obedience to him, and to keep his commands, decrees and laws; then you will live and increase, and the LORD your God will bless you in the land you are entering to possess. Dt 30:16* Let you and I Harken to His voice.

LET'S PRAY TOGETHER:
Lord, open my spiritual eyes, as you did with Elijah's servant *in 2 Kings 6*. Change my heart so I can see your truth as your prophets have written it, inspired by you.

Fill my life with peace, strength, and courage to be able to walk in obedience, that every moment that you give me, that I will take the opportunity to proclaim your word everywhere I go. You are the Redeemer of Israel, may I always be ready to say yes just as The Virgin Mary, your mother did. This I ask in the name that is above every name Christ Jesus. Amen!

ACTION STEPS:
Begin a new life in Christ, even if we are already walking with Him, there is always space for expansion & growth; recognize His Holy Spirit leaves in you.

Spend time in the sacred scriptures, meditate on the following verse and ask the Lord to renew your mind.

Therefore, brothers and sisters, considering the mercy of God, I pray that each of you, in spiritual adoration, offer his body as a living sacrifice, holy and pleasing to God. Do not conform to today's world but be transformed by renewing your mind. In this way they will be able to verify what is the will of God, good, pleasant, and perfect. Rom 12;1,2

JHWH / YAHWEH
EHYÉ-ASHER-EHYÉ

"The Great I AM."

Then Moses said to God, "Behold, when I come to the Israelites and say to them, 'The God of your fathers (ancestors) has sent me to you,' and they say to me, 'What is His name?' What shall I say to them?" God said to Moses, "I Am Who I Am"; and He said, "You shall say this to the Israelites, 'I Am has sent me to you.'" Then God also said to Moses, "This is what you shall say to the Israelites, 'The Lord, the God of your fathers, the God of Abraham, the God of Isaac, and the God of Jacob (Israel), has sent me to you.' This is My Name forever, and this is My memorial [name] to all generations.

Exodus 3:13-15 (AMP)

UNWRAPPING THE MIRACLE WITHIN

Elisha said to her, "What shall I do for you? Tell me, what do you have [of value] in the house?" She said, "Your maidservant has nothing in the house except a [small] jar of [olive] oil."

2 King 4:2 (AMP)

REFLECTION:

Elisha asks the widow, a pivotal question, that its diminishing and undermining answer release increased to turn her life around forever. Many times, we fail to recognize what we already possess.

The widow could and would have brought a devastating result of slavery to her children, if she only would have forgotten what was in her house and in her power. But she remembered there was an insignificant little amount of oil. Yet, with faith and obedience she listened to the prophet and her hidden treasure was unleashed, overflowing with abundance.

The widow's story teaches us to seek guidance from those in a close relationship with God, who can point us to supernatural solutions. But we can't forget that we too can come directly to Christ; and speak with Him. Remember we now have access to Christ, He has destroyed the separation that kept us from Him.

Very often, we seek outside solutions, forgetting the still small voice within *1 King 19:12* guiding us. There to teach us every step of our journey. God has a miracle with your name written on it, just waiting to be unwrapped and taken a hold of, today and now.

Our dependence upon others doesn't always guarantee the solutions to our problems. Just like the paralyzed man in Bethesda's story in *Jn 5:5,9,* we may be waiting for someone else to help us, instead of turning our focus to Jesus, our provider.

Yes, God has His Prophets and angels ready to attend to our needs, but He is a prayer away *Jer 33:3*. He has already prepared solutions beforehand *Eph 2:10*. Just like the centurion in *Lk 7:7*, was able to recognize Jesus's authority here on earth, we too can trust in His word alone to shift our situations forever.

The enemy seeks to destroy our families, marriages, children, businesses, and livelihoods, but our sovereign King Jesus, has already provided miracles awaiting its manifestation for you and me. Let us go to the sacred place, seeking guidance from His Spirit, and trusting in His power and might through us.

Our miracles are at the door, ready to flow abundantly into our lives. Let us unwrap the hidden blessing within us to receive His treasures.

LET'S PRAY TOGETHER:

Dear Heavenly Father, I come before you with faith, and expectation, knowing that my miracle is found in Your presence, Oh **Great I AM!** You are self-existent, unchanging, and all powerful. Your promises are yes and amen, and I claim them over my life right now.

Jesus, the true vine, you are the way, the truth, and life. I accept the master key of Your revelations and the power of Your name to destroy the enemy's evil plans. I know that You are the only God, and demons tremble at the mention of Your name Jm 2:19.

Set me free with Your truths, Your promises will bring manifestation to my prayers and peace to my soul. Faithful Father. In Jesus' name, I pray. Amen.

ACTION STEPS:

Take time to read and reflect on scriptures like Isaiah 53 for illness, Psalm 127 for parenting struggles, Matthew 19:6 for marital challenges, and Joshua 24:15 for your household and generation to come.

Allow God's promises and truths to sink deep into your heart and mind.

Speak out loud the word of God. Meditate on His promises believe them, knowing that your circumstances are temporary.

YAHWEH MEFALTI

"The Lord my Deliverer"

"I love You [fervently and devotedly], O Lord, my strength."
The Lord is my rock, my fortress, and the One
who rescues me; My God, my rock and strength in whom
I trust and take refuge; My shield, and the horn of my
salvation, my high tower—my stronghold.

Psalms 18:1-2 (AMP)

UNDISPUTABLE BLOOD POWER

For the Lord will pass through to strike the Egyptians; and when He sees the blood on the lintel [above the entryway] and on the two doorposts, the Lord will pass over the door and will not allow the destroyer to come into your houses to slay you.

Exodus 12:23

REFLECTION:

Welcome to a day of triumph and victory! Today, we remember the ancient miracle of the Passover. Where the blood on the lintel and doorposts of their homes served as a sign and saved the Israelites from destruction. But we also celebrate a far greater truth: the shed blood of Jesus Christ, which spares us from eternal destruction and equips us to conquer the enemy's schemes.

Through Jesus' blood, we have been redeemed, protected, and empowered to overcome.

Let us embrace the undisputable power of His sacrifice and walk in the freedom and victory bought for us. May this day be a declaration of our faith, a testimony to the immeasurable power of Jesus' blood, and a triumph over the forces of darkness.

I received this revelation early on, in my journey with Jesus around 2007. I want to emphasize the importance of Jesus's blood because with the awareness of its powerful redemption we can bind, neutralize, and annihilate demonic powers. Jesus redeemed us from the enemy's grasp *Eph 1:7.*

In the Old Testament, the blood of an unblemished animal represented Jesus' blood, giving us protection against the destroyer. *Ex 12:13-14.*

Today, we have a new *covenant. Lk 22:20* and it has accomplished a mightier power. We are to spiritually apply it with the knowledge of what it has already provided for you and me. *His blood speaks a better thing for us, Heb 12:24, overcoming Satan. "And they overcame and conquered him because of the blood of the Lamb and because of the word of their testimony, for they did not love their life and renounce their faith even when faced with death. Rev 12:11*

Through faith in His blood, we can take a hold off the deliverance, salvation, redemption, and the complete pardon from sin, Jesus paid for. Though troubles will come *John 16:33*, the blood of Jesus remains effective, making demons flee instantly.

I have pleaded Jesus's blood over countless situations for many years as God is my witness. I have seen the changes take place right before my eyes.

Remember, to walk under His full protection, we must be doers of His word. James 1:23-24, living according to His will. Always, willing to share your testimonies boldly.

LET'S PRAY TOGETHER:

"Beloved Father, **YAHWEH MEFALTI**, my Deliverer and Redeemer, I come before you today with gratitude and faith. I know that your precious blood has redeemed me and washed me white as snow. It has already saved me and my family from the snares of the enemy.

Heavenly Father, I ask for your forgiveness if I have done wrong against you and your people. I cover each of my generations from my maternal side as well as those of my paternal side with your blood shed on the Cross of Calvary. Today any ancestral chains are broken.

I apologize for those who passed without accepting you in my family and from now on and forever, as for me and my household we will serve the Lord. I place your eternal law ahead of all my present and future generations.

For the L ORD *will pass through the land to strike down the Egyptians. But when he sees the blood on the top and sides of the doorframe, the* L ORD *will pass over your home. He will not permit his death angel to enter your house and strike you down. Remember, these instructions are a permanent law that you and your descendants must observe forever. Exodus 12:23,24.* Thank you, Lord. Amen!!

ACTION STEPS:

Today begins a new cycle of blessing and protection for your life. Believe and trust that you are under the new covenant of His blood, and teach your children and or your loved ones to do the same.

Plead the blood over your family. Sample; my husband doesn't leave the house until I speak and apply the blood of Jesus over him from the top of his head to the bottom of his feet, I also include everything Jesus has given us.

If you haven't done it already, do it now. There is power in proclaiming the precious blood of Jesus with your own words. I (your name here) plead the blood of Jesus to cover, shield and to serve as protection over my life. Come on. Speak it!

When facing challenges or difficulties, apply the blood of Jesus by faith, knowing that His blood has overcome Satan *Rev 12:11.* Believe the power of His blood will bring freedom, peace, and victory.

Fearlessly share your testimony, knowing you've already conquered. Remember, applying the blood of Jesus is a spiritual act with tangible power. By faith, plead it in your life.

ELOHE TSADEKI

"God of my Justice"

When I call, give me answers.
God, take my side! Once, in a tight place,
you gave me room; Now I'm in trouble again:
grace me! hear me!

Psalms 4:1 (MSG)

UNDER THE SHEPHERD'S CARE

The Lord is my shepherd, I lack nothing. He makes me lie down in green pastures, He leads me beside quiet waters, He refreshes my soul. He guides me along the right paths for his name's sake. Even though I walk through the darkest valley,[a] I will fear no evil, for you are with me; your rod and your staff, they comfort me. You prepare a table before me in the presence of my enemies. You anoint my head with oil; my cup overflows. Surely your goodness and love will follow me all the days of my life and I will dwell in the house of the Lord forever.

Psalm 23 (NIV)

REFLECTION:

"Today, we're reminded that our lives need guidance beyond a simple compass. We need a Shepherd who cares for our well-being, defends us from predators, and loves us unconditionally. Jesus, our Good Shepherd, knows our vulnerabilities and the attacks of the enemy. But He assures us, 'I will never leave you nor forsake you' *Heb 13:5.*

In times of trouble, we may feel like lost sheep, but God's love and mercy are not based on our worthiness. He loves us because of who He is, not who we are. He sent His Son to save us, not condemn us *John 3:16-17.* Remember, God is our loving Father, and His Holy Spirit will guide us. His love is not based on our past or present but on His greatness and mercy. Let's come to Him with confidence, knowing He's always on our side.

As His sheep we just got to be laser focused on Him who has called us by name. Let's read how Peter puts it; *1 Peter 5:8 Be alert and of sober mind. Your enemy the devil prowls around like a roaring lion looking for someone to devour.* But don't forget we are not at the enemy's mercy, we have the good Shepherd that cares for us.

We have this assurance in Christ. *Matt 18:12-14 "What do you think? If a man has a hundred sheep, and one of them gets lost, will he not leave the ninety-nine on the mountain and go in search of the one that is lost? And if it turns out that he finds it, I assure you and most solemnly say to you, he rejoices over it more than over the ninety-nine that did not get lost. So, it is not the will of your Father who is in heaven that one of these little ones be lost."* Wow!

This brings up a memory of a difficult season in my life, there are too many to even count. This time God sent an angel named Silene Rosa from New York to Florida to my rescue. I had briefly met her once at a prayer circle and I kept her contact, after praying with me a couple of times over the phone. God moved Silene with this verse in *Matthew 18* to fly over to Florida to give me a word of encouragement. I needed it so much.

I couldn't believe she left everything behind to come and meet me, she asked for nothing in return, not even for the plane ticket. Silene simply was obedient to what Jesus had put in her heart. I will forever be thankful for her life. We now have an outstanding friendship. I'm sure the Holy Spirit inspired me through her to become a missionary. Today I leave everything behind to go and serve the unserved overseas. You too can make a change in someone's life. Join me today at GR Eternal Foundation Inc a nonprofit organization to serve the needy nationwide.

LET'S PRAY TOGETHER:
"Dear Heavenly Father, ELOHE TSADEKI, we come before you today with humble hearts. We pray for those who feel lost and far from you, that they may be found by Jesus, our Good Shepherd. May we be the connecting bridge that leads them to Your love and grace. I pray for the revelation of the wounds you received to heal me, so that I may become whole. Help me recognize Your presence in my life.

May we be light in the darkness, sharing Your peace that surpasses all understanding. *Ph 4:7 Then you will experience God's peace, which exceeds anything we can understand. His peace will guard your hearts and minds as you live in Christ Jesus.* I pray in Jesus's name. Amen!

ACTION STEPS:

Share Jesus' love and grace with someone who may be lost or struggling today.

Ask God to reveal and heal any wounds or areas of darkness in your life, ask the same for the life of others.

Offer support and guidance to someone who needs connection and direction. Meditate on John 14:27, and receive God's peace today.

LUMINOUS DAY 18

ELOHIM KEDOSHIM

"GOD IS HOLY"

And the four living creatures, each one of them having six wings, are full of eyes all over and within [underneath their wings]; and day and night they never stop saying, "Holy, holy, holy [is the] Lord God, the Almighty [the Omnipotent, the Ruler of all], who was and who is and who is to come [the unchanging, eternal God]."

Revelation 4:8 (AMP)

FROM DECLARATION TO DESTINATION

*If you declare with your mouth, "Jesus is Lord,"
and believe in your heart that God raised him
from the dead, you will be saved.*

Romans 10:9 (NIV)

REFLECTION:

"Today, we embark on a luminous journey, declaring Jesus as Lord and Savior. This newfound faith ignites a transformation process, where our spirit man discovers divine plans tailored for us since creation.

Though our outer nature may still struggle with imperfections, God's grace perfects us daily *Phil 1:6* Our spirit man is on the road to discover the divine plans the Lord has set apart for you and I, since before the foundation of the earth.

Yes, the word of God assures us that when we invite Him to dwell in our lives, we become new creatures, *2 Cor 5:17 Therefore, if anyone is in Christ, the new creation has come: The old has gone, the new is here!*

As we continue the game of life, we're reminded that our journey is not a solo endeavor. Christ Himself walked the path, overcoming the world's obstacles *John 16:33* We're assured that our struggles are not unique, and God's peace can conquer the turbulence we might face.

Many years ago, I received this revelation as I began to travel more, the Christian life is often likened to a plane's journey. We start with a declaration of faith, like boarding a plane. As we progress, we encounter processes and trials, just like the security checks and turbulence during a flight. But, unlike the temporary nature of a plane ride, our walk with God is a lifelong journey. Confess Him today!

On this walk, we're called to holiness as we are set apart for God's purposes *1 Peter 1:16*. The Holy Spirit, our helper, guides us towards perfection. *Jn 14:18, 26*. We're not alone in our struggles; God's love and grace accompany us every step of the way.

But you and I have a command, *And he said to them all, If any man will come after me, let him deny himself, and take up his cross daily, and follow me. LK 9:23* I know most of us await our retirement season but wait, the journey isn't over yet. Our destination is In Christ, life continues until we are called back home to be with the Lord in His mansion where He has a room for you and I.

God provided a way for sinful humanity to draw near to Him through the sacrifice of Christ, by the shedding of His blood on the Cross. .

LET'S PRAY TOGETHER:
Dear Heavenly Father, ELOHE TSADEKI, I come before you today, declaring Jesus as my Lord and Savior. Help me understand that my journey is not my own, but yours, and I want to surrender to your divine plans. I want to walk in holiness, set apart for your purposes. Guide me through the processes and fill me with your peace.

Thank you for the gift of the Holy Spirit. May my lives radiate your love and grace to a world in need. Illuminate my understanding, that I may know your mysteries and plans for my life. Renew my mind and let it be transformed by your love. In Jesus' name I pray. Amen!

ACTION STEPS:
Ask God to illuminate your understanding, revealing His truth and plans for your life's journey.

Praise the Lord daily, it helps especially in times of trouble.

Strive for holiness, set yourself apart, despite life's challenges.

Study God's word, renewing your mind with wisdom and understanding.

72

LUMINOUS DAY 19

EL ROI

"GOD WHO SEES"

Then she called the name of the Lord who spoke to her, "You are God Who Sees"; for she said, "Have I not even here [in the wilderness] remained alive after seeing Him [who sees me with understanding and compassion]?"

Genesis 16:13 (AMP)

SPIRITUAL EYES

*Then Elisha prayed and said, "Lord, please,
open his eyes that he may see." And the Lord opened
the servant's eyes and he saw; and behold, the mountain
was full of horses and chariots of fire surrounding Elisha.*

2 Kings 6:17 (AMP)

REFLECTION:

Today, we stand at the threshold of a divine revelation. We are reminded of the importance of our spiritual eyes in the unseen realm surrounding us. Just as Elisha prayed for his servant's eyes to be opened, we too must ask God the same thing for ourselves. We too need to learn to walk by faith, not by sight. Our bodies are temporary shells, but our spirit man is eternal.

As we navigate through life's challenges, we must remember that we're in a spiritual battle. The enemy seeks to distract us from God's truth and blind us with deceptions and illusions of the reality we face. But God's word is a powerful double-edged weapon, and prayer is our direct line to connect with Him.

Psalm 91 for example has been a powerful shield of protection for me and it has been a source of comfort and strength in times of warfare, since I was a little girl. The scripture reminds us that God is our refuge and our fortress, a God in whom we can trust. A thousand may fall at your side and ten thousand behind you but with God on your side they won't harm you.

May we hunger for more of Jesus and meditate on His words day and night, as it builds our faith and trust in His promises.

We are commended in the book of Joshua 1:8 that the word of God should always be present in our lives. *This Book of the Law shall not depart from your mouth, but you shall read [and meditate on] its day and night, so that you may be careful to do [everything] in accordance with all that is written in it; for then you will make your way prosperous, and then you will be successful.*

The book of Hebrews 4:12 confirms us how powerful that truly is. *For the word of God is alive and active. Sharper than any double-edged sword, it penetrates even to dividing soul and spirit, joints and marrow; it judges the thoughts and attitudes of the heart.* God's word builds our faith if we diligently seek it.

Just as the servant's eyes were opened to see the horses and chariots of fire surrounding them in times of trouble. Our eyes too can be opened to see God's glory and power working in and around us, to see there is more with us than against us.

LET'S PRAY TOGETHER:

Father, you are the all-seeing and all-knowing God, you chose me before I was born. David tells us in *Psalms 139:7 & 13 Where can I go from Your Spirit? Or where can I flee from Your presence?–For You formed my innermost parts; You knit me [together] in my mother's womb.* Oh Lord! praises to your holy name throughout the earth.

Lord Jesus: I ask you to open my spiritual eyes so that I can see you working through me and in my environment. Holy Spirit guide, help me recognize that you live on the inside of me and you have given me the authority to be able to work on your behalf here on earth. All this I ask in the mighty name of Jesus, Amen!

ACTION STEPS:

Live your life consistent with your belief in God's promises, not by what you see.

Ask Him to give you spiritual eyes to see beyond this earthly realm.

Seek to have an intimate relationship with Jesus.

Ask for wisdom and discernment to understand the spiritual realities. Search for His presence and guidance in your life.

ELOHIM OZER LI

"GOD IS MY HELPER"

Behold, God is my helper and ally;
The Lord is the sustainer of my soul [my upholder].

Psalms 54:4 (AMP

SOWING SEEDS OF COMPASSION

Do not withhold good from those to whom it is due
[its rightful recipients], When it is in your power to do it.

Proverbs 3:27 (AMP)

REFLECTION:

Today, we're reminded that compassion is not just a feeling, but a choice. A choice to sow seeds of kindness, empathy, and generosity into the lives of others.

When we withhold good from those who need it, we're not only hurting them, but also ourselves. We're essentially drying up the soil of our own hearts, making it almost impossible for any sustainable harvest to grow.

Yes there are consequences when the opportunity presents itself to share with others but we decide not to do it, and simply walk away in disobedience.

What does Jesus tell us in this matter: *Mat 25;42,46 For I was hungry and you gave me nothing to eat, I was thirsty and you gave me nothing to drink, I was a stranger and you did not invite me in, I needed clothes and you did not clothe me, I was sick and in prison and you did not look after me. They also will answer, 'Lord, when did we see you hungry or thirsty or a stranger or needing clothes or sick or in prison, and did not help you? He will reply, 'Truly I tell you, whatever you did not do for one of the least of these, you did not do for me.' Then they will go away to eternal punishment, but the righteous to eternal life.*

Yes, when you do it for them you do it for God. And that creates a ripple effect of kindness that can impact our lives for generations to come. The best part is we progressively get closer to inherit eternal life.

We rarely consider this, but every act of compassion is an act of self-preservation. When we show mercy to others, we're actually saving ourselves from the corrosive effects of bitterness, anger, and resentment.

Look for opportunities to show kindness, to listen, to understand, and to help. Let's create a world where everyone can flourish, yes that includes you and me. We can create a more loving, more just, and more peaceful world – one act of kindness at a time.

Don't concern yourself with how others will use what you give them; let God deal with that. Our responsibility is to obey Him and love others as He loves us.

LET'S PRAY TOGETHER:
Lord teach me to be a cheerful giver, that everything I do, I do for you Jesus. *Whatever you do, work at it with all your heart, as working for the Lord, not for human masters, since you know that you will receive an inheritance from the Lord as a reward. It is the Lord Christ you are serving. Col 3:23-24*

ELOHIM OZER LI, help me learn to be a doer of your word and not just a listener of it. *for once he has looked at himself and gone away, he immediately forgets what he looked like. But he who looks carefully into the perfect law, the law of liberty, and faithfully abides by it, not having become a [careless] listener who forgets but an active doer [who obeys], he will be blessed and favored by God in what he does [in his life of obedience]. James 1:22-25*

Father, I want to be a financier of your kingdom, to lend and not to borrow. Guide me to attend to the needs of those who most need the help, this I ask in the powerful name of Jesus. Amen!!

ACTION STEPS:
Share your resources, time, and talents with others. Look for a person to show kindness to each day, all they might need is a listening ear.

Put yourself in other people's shoes and try to understand their struggles. Listen to the Holy Spirit's guidance and obey His instructions. Trust God to deal with the consequences of your actions, and don't worry about how others will use what you've give them.

Experience through serving and sharing the grace and love that comes from obeying God and don't forget to give Him the glory.

YAHWEH ELOHE ABOTHEKEM

"The Lord, God of your fathers"

*So, Joshua asked them, "How long will you put
off entering to take possession of the land which the Lord,
the God of your fathers, has given you?*

Joshua 18:3 (AMP)

GRATITUDE: A GATEWAY TO GOD'S GOODNESS

Let them give thanks to the Lord for His lovingkindness, And for His wonderful acts to the children of men! For He satisfies the parched throat And fills the hungry appetite with what is good.

Psalms 107:8-9 (amp)

REFLECTION:

The Psalmist calls us to give thanks to the Lord for His lovingkindness and wonderful acts. But what if our thanksgiving is not just a reaction to what God has done, but a declaration of who He is? What if our gratitude is not just a feeling, but a statement of faith? In short you and I should live with our hearts filled with gratitude and thanksgiving, a lifestyle that describes our essence.

Gratitude is a key to unlocking God's miracles, signs and wonders. When we cultivate a thankful mindset, we open ourselves a gateway of His goodness. Again, here's a truth we rarely consider: our gratitude is not just a response to God's greater goodness and compassion, but a declaration of our identity of His image and likeness in our daily lives.

This truth only takes root in our lives when we embrace a thankful heart. When we thank God, we're not just acknowledging supernatural events we have encountered; we're affirming our position as beloved children, joint heirs with Christ, you and I were not worthy of His love and favor. But God so loved the world that He gave His only son up so we would not perish but rather have eternal life in Him.

Glory be to God! We are his workmanship! *The earth is the Lord's, and the fullness of it, the world, and those who dwell in it. Psalms. 24:1,*

Yes, He loved you and I then, loves you and I now and will always love us for all eternity. You and I are the apple of his eye. Let us thank God for His love, for His mercy and for all His wonders for the children of men. He is **YAHWEH ELOHE ABOTHEKEM,** the God of our ancestors and He has left us an inheritance and wants us to possess it today.

The kingdom of God is among us, looking to be manifested in our daily lives. Begin every morning with a thankful heart, speak it and declare it from the rooftop!

LET'S PRAY TOGETHER:
Holy Spirit teach me to start my days with a thankful heart. Let me proclaim the works of your hands, your love and kindness. Today I choose wisely! *As for me and my house, we will serve the Lord. Joshua 24;15*

Glory to God in the highest! I want to praise your name every day for the rest of my life. Father, give me the revelation of what it means to be a son- daughter that carries your image on the inside as a shield impregnated in my soul and spirit. Jesus grant me your joy, that I may share it wherever I go and with those I encounter. All this I ask in your mighty name Jesus of Nazareth. Amen!

ACTION STEPS:
Make thanksgiving a lifestyle, not just a reaction. Thank God for who He is in you, not just what He has done or will do.

Embrace your position as a joint heir with Christ, affirm His lovingkindness and provision in your life.

Learn to have a constant thankful heart it will unlock a floodgate of blessings and you will experience the fullness of His inheritance here on earth.

LUMINOUS DAY 22

YAHWEH CHEREB

"The Lord the Sword"

*"Happy and blessed are you, O Israel; Who is like you,
a people saved by the Lord, The Shield of your help,
And the Sword of your majesty! Your enemies will cringe
before you, And you will tread on their high places
[tramping down their idolatrous altars]."*

Deuteronomy 33:29 (AMP)

A CONNECTION WITH HEAVEN

*Praying always with all prayer and supplication
in the Spirit, being watchful to this end with all
perseverance and supplication for all the saints.*

Ephesians 6:18 (NKJV)

REFLECTION:

Today, we're reminded that prayer is not just a traditional ritual or a 1 2 3 list of prayers we repeat unceasingly, but a powerful tool to access God's presence and through that we then encounter His provisions. We're not begging God for what Jesus has already paid for, we're simply aligning ourselves with His will and receiving what's already ours.

Prayer It's also about watching and waiting. It's about being vigilant and persevering, even when the answers seem delayed. It's about trusting that God is working behind the scenes, overseeing His master plan for our lives. It's putting our faith on His promises and believing He is faithful to perform the deeds of His mouth.

Our prayers are not just about us; they're about God's larger plan to bless others through us. When we pray, we should not only be seeking our own interests; but rather we should be on the path looking for how to partner with God, to bring His kingdom to earth as it is in heaven for all humanity.

Two important parts about prayer are pointed out in the verse and that is that we are to pray in the spirit and to persevere.

It is extremely essential to pray with intention and purpose, we cannot start by repeating words that can be blown away by the wind as soon as they come out of our mouths. Let us ask the Holy Spirit to help us persevere and to baptize us and teach us to pray in the spirit with tongues of fire.

Praying in the Spirit is a game-changer, a direct connection with heaven. It's not just about speaking words; but rather connecting with our counselor The Holy Spirit, who knows our deepest needs and desires. When we pray in the Spirit, we're not limited by our own understanding; we're tapping into God's infinite wisdom and power.

But it was to us that God revealed these things by his Spirit. For his Spirit searches out everything and shows us God's deep secrets. 1 Cor 2:10

We must learn that prayer is not a magic pill, Prayers are a direct connection with heaven, a lifestyle that invites us and leads us to have a personal relationship with our creator and His Holy Ghost, a daily communion from father to son and daughter. Let us be vigilant!

LET'S PRAY TOGETHER:

I am not alone nor helpless, Jesus has not left me orphan, I am part of God's chosen people, He is my shield and my sword. What else can I say that if God is with me, nothing and no one can oppose what He already has in store for my life.

My dear Jesus, on this day I want to present myself as a useful instrument in your presence, take me as a pleasing offering to you. May your Holy Spirit be my guidance, helping me to renew my mind through the revelations of the scriptures. I am willing to connect with you spiritually to pray and worship you in spirit and in truth *John 4:24* so that I can see miracles and wonders in my life and that of my loved ones. Teach me to intercede for the whole world in prayer especially for those who need and yearn to know you and accept you as their Savior. I ask this in the mighty name of Jesus. Amen!

ACTION STEPS:

So, let's not just pray when we need something; let's pray because we want to know God personally. Let's pray because we want to experience the fullness of His presence and power in our lives.

Connect spiritually as you pray in the Spirit. Be vigilant and persevering in your prayers, trusting God's timing and plan.

Seek and prioritize having an intimate relationship with God and let the Spirit drive your prayers. Meditating in the world of God is a must in our daily routine.

YAHWEH-NISSI

"God my Banner"

Then the Lord said to Moses, "Write this in the book as a memorial and recite it to Joshua, that I will utterly wipe out the memory of Amalek [and his people] from under heaven." And Moses built an altar and named it The Lord Is My Banner.

Exodus 17:14,15 (AMP)

UNLOCKING THE POWER OF BELIEVING

*And whatever you ask for in prayer,
believing, you will receive."*

Mathew 21:22 (AMP)

REFLECTION:

Today, we're reminded that our God is a supernatural God, capable of accomplishing what seems impossible. Yet, many of us struggle to tap into this power due to the lack of awareness, limited understanding and doubting minds.

This main verse holds a master key: believing. It's the ingredient that unlocks God's provision and turns our circumstances around. But believing requires knowing the creator personally, trust, surrender and a willingness to override doubts during contrary circumstances.

On a recent mission trip to the Dominican Republic in November of 2023 I experienced a tough situation where I became extremely ill as soon as I set my feet at the airport on my way back home. I literally thought I was going to die that day. I even entrusted John, my traveling partner, he was 12 at that time, on what to do if I took too long in the bathroom.

But in the face of adversity, I began to plead the blood over my situation and I kept believing and telling myself Claribel you will be ok, this is temporary, you shall live and not die. In the mists of my pain and confusion I reminded myself that God had shown me places I hadn't been nor seen yet.

Despite initial setbacks and frustrations during my 5 and half hour flights, I chose to shift my focus and pray. In doing so, I regained peace and experienced God's supernatural intervention. We must recognize that *our battles are not against flesh and blood*, but against evil spiritual forces. *Eph 6:12.*

Here's the truth: our human efforts alone cannot manifest what *Matthew 21:22* is talking about. The receiving part of its manifestation is all dependent on your believing faith in Christ. You must truly believe who He is and that He is a *rewarder of those who diligently seek Him. Heb 11:6*

Think of believing like adding the final ingredients to your favorite recipe. Without it, the dish remains incomplete. Similarly, without believing, our prayers and efforts remain ineffective.

God is no respecter of persons, He assures us that all good and perfect gifts come from Him. Jesus Christ remains the same yesterday, today, and forever, His supernatural power is available to us, regardless of our circumstances.

LET'S PRAY TOGETHER:
O Heavenly Father, *Bless the Lord, O my soul, and do not forget any of His benefits.* Teach me Lord, to believe in your wonders and know that you always listen to me, that you are attentive to my prayers and ready to answer them if I believe it shall be.

Jesus, may I not be deaf or blinded to your truth let me not be deceived. Deliver me from the tricks of satan, may he never again influence my mind.

For I declare I have the mind of Christ. Thank you, for I know I have victory in You, having the certainty that *this battle is not mine, but yours Lord. 2 Chr. 20:15* All this I ask in the mighty name of Jesus. ¡Amen!

Action Steps:

Override contrary circumstances and trust God's super power.

Shift Your Focus, Redirect your attention to blessing others in the midst of challenges. Actively engage in prayer

Acknowledge your weakness but stand firm on God's strength in you.

Remember His Faithfulness, Reflect on God's past interventions in your life. Declare and Speak God's truth and promises over your circumstances and step out in obedience, trusting God's supernatural guidance.

LUMINOUS DAY 24

JEHOVAH JIREH

"The Lord will Provide."

*So, Abraham named that place
The Lord Will Provide. And it is said to this day,
"On the mountain of the Lord it will be seen and provided."*

Génesis 22:14 (AMP)

YIELDING A FRUITFUL HARVEST

*"I assure you and most solemnly say to you,
unless a grain of wheat falls into the earth and dies,
it remains alone [just one grain, never more]. But if it dies,
it produces much grain and yields a harvest."*

John 12:24 (AMP)

REFLECTION:

A spiritual death to our old sinful nature it's a necessary change to embrace a new life, for the purpose that God has called us to. Just as a grain of wheat must die to produce a harvest, we too must surrender our old selves to experience resurrection power.

In *2 Corinthians 5:17*, we're assured that anyone in Christ becomes a new person, leaving the old life behind. This transformation enables us to bear fruit for God's kingdom. *John 15:4-5* reinforces this truth, illustrating our dependence on Christ, the vine, in order for the branches to produce fruit we must stay in Him, apart *from Him we cannot do anything.*

As we navigate challenging times globally, remember that these difficulties will pass. You and I were created with a divine purpose, and we have to walk by faith and not by what we see that surrounds us. Those who trust in God will persevere, receiving eternal life.

The grain of wheat's death is not in vain; it yields a harvest for God's ultimate purpose. We're called to die to the flesh, embracing our new spiritual life through Christ.

This purpose is to:
- Bring hope to the needy
- Encourage the discouraged
- Liberate the oppressed

- Feed the hungry
- Heal the sick
- Set the captives free
- Shine the light to push darkness out
- Bring truth in the midst of confusion

Let go of prejudices, accusations, and judgmental thinking. Jesus is the judge! God's ways are not ours. He acts with mercy, according to His divine plans.

The parable of the weeds and wheat teaches us: The importance of growth alongside challenges. God will ultimately separate good and evil, His promises of a fruitful harvest is for those who persevere. **YAHWEH JIREH** our savior and our provider is for us.

LET'S PRAY TOGETHER:

Abba Father, I know and trust that *You will meet all of my needs according to your riches in glory*. You are the God who provides for all your children and their generations. The purpose for which you created me will come to fruition as I am a new creation in you. We are told in your word in *Mark 4:8 "And other seeds fell into good soil, and as the plants grew and increased, they yielded a crop and produced thirty, sixty, and a hundred times [as much as had been sown]."*

Lord, I trust that what you have deposited in me will give a great harvest according to your call and divine plan in me. Today I ask that You increase in my life so that I can decrease. That I may sing praises to your Holy name. I ask all this in the name of Yeshua hamashiach the Anointed One of Israel. Lord bless your people, protect Israel from all harmful attacks! Amen!

ACTION STEPS:

Surrender your old nature and embrace the spiritual resurrection power now.

Abide in Christ, remain in Him, you will produce fruit for God's kingdom. Have faith in His divine strategies for your life. As you have received, give unto others, share hope, encouragement, and liberty.

Trust The Holy Spirit as your guidance and the blood of Jesus as your protection.

GIBBOR MILCHAMAH

"The Mighty Lord in Battle"

Who is the King of glory?
The Lord strong and mighty,
The Lord mighty in battle.

Psalm 24:8 (AMP)

WINGS OF PROTECTION

*I live in the shelter of the Most High I am under His shadow.
This I declare about the LORD: He alone is my refuge,
my place of safety. He is my God, and I trust Him. For He
will rescue me from every trap and protect me from deadly disease. His faithful promises are my armor and protection.
I will not be afraid of the terrors of the night, nor the arrow that
flies in the day. I will not dread the disease that stalks in darkness, nor the disaster that strikes at midday. Though a thousand fall at my side, though ten thousand are dying around me,
these evils will not touch me. When I open my eyes, I see
how the wicked are punished. Because I make the LORD
my refuge, Because I make the Most High my shelter, No evil
will conquer me; no plague will come near my home. For He
will order His angels to protect me wherever I go. They will
hold me up with their hands so I won't even hurt my foot on a
stone. I'll trample upon lions and cobras; I'll crush fierce lions
and serpents under my feet! The LorD says, "I will rescue those
who love Me. I will protect those who trust in My name.
When they call on Me, I will answer; I will be with them in
trouble. I will rescue and honor them. I will reward them with
a long life and give them My salvation.?*

Psalm 91 (NLT) Personalized

REFLECTION:

You and I can abide under God's unwavering wings of protection
and all His promises in Psalm 91. This powerful prayer has been
a beacon of hope and strength for me since my childhood when
I didn't even imagine serving the Lord, never mind knowing Him.
Jesus placed a shield of protection over me, as I encountered
nightmares, fears, and uncertainties during those young years.
That's when I learned this scripture by heart.

As I reflect on my journey, I realize that God was preparing me to
trust in His sacred scriptures, even when I didn't fully understand

nor did I know them except for this Psalm. He engraved His Word on my heart, empowering me to face challenges with faith and courage as I recited it.

My story is a testimony to the transformative power of faith and trust in the sacred scriptures. From childhood nightmares to spiritual awakening, Psalm 91 has been my anchor, reminding me of God's constant presence and protection. It can be yours too, if you commit to it as daily prayer as I have. Remember even if you don't feel anything at the beginning, continue to trust you will see victory if you stay in faith through your praying life. Climb and maintain your course, don't back down. The devil is a liar and he is trying to make you and I believe that our circumstances are not temporary, but we can walk by faith knowing God is faithful.

Some promises for those who dwell in the shelter of the Most High:
- Rescue and protection from harm
- Safety from traps and snares
- Coverage under His wings
- God's truth will be your shield and buckler
- You won't fear the terror of night or the arrow that flies by day nor the plague that destroys at midday
- Angels will guard you in all your ways
- With long life, God will satisfy you
- God will call you His own and answer when you call
- Romans 8:31 reminds us, *If God is for us, who can be against us?* With God on our side, we are unstoppable and unbreakable.

Let us glorify His holy name, and may His protection be our constant companion.

LET'S PRAY TOGETHER:

Dear Lord, allow me to perceive your presence and divine protection every day. I place all my fears of all that concerns me and my generations in your powerful hands, *Psalm 103:17 But the lovingkindness of the Lord is from everlasting to everlasting on those who [reverently] fear Him, And His righteousness to His children's children.* Jesus, I trust in you!

May your word never leave my mouth, may I always remember that you are my shield and my strength, the mighty God in battle. Send your angels to the land of Israel as they endure this war, cover, shield and protect your people inside and outside their territory with your precious blood that was shed on the cross. I pray that all the nations of the earth are protected from the schemes of the enemy and that we can turn our faces towards you in repentance. Bring us all into your truth Jesus as you are the truth. I ask this in the name that is above every name Christ Jesus. Amen!

ACTION STEPS:

Embed Psalm 91 in your heart, reciting it daily and believe in His protection and care.

Call upon God's angels for guidance and safety and step into challenges with confidence in God's presence.

Remember, God's mercy endures forever. His shelter is our refuge, and His promises are our armor.

EL SIMCHATH GILI

"God, my Joy Overflowing"

I will go to the altar of God, To God, my exceeding joy;
With the lyre I will praise You, O God, my God!

Psalms 43:4 (AMP)

JOURNEY WITH THE HOLY SPIRIT

*Rejoice always, pray continually, give thanks
in all circumstances; for this is God's will for you in
Christ Jesus. Do not quench the Spirit*

1 Thessalonians 5:16-19 (NIV)

REFLECTION:

I would like to emphasize the last line in today's verse; Do *not quench the Spirit*. This should serve as a powerful reminder for you and I. In my minimal understanding of life I could truly see how one who ardently walks in such a way as to not quenching the Spirit of God could walk thumpingly every day.

My personal testimony echoes this truth, please understand in any way shape or form am I saying I'm a perfect human being, I am a work in progress every day of my life.

Many years ago, as a single mother, I faced darkness, fears and many uncertainties. The shadows of doubt crept in, threatening to extinguish the flame of my hope. Yet, in the midst of chaos, the Lord's presence was my fortress, my refuge, and my guiding light. God's Spirit kept guiding me, I'm sure at times when I had no idea it was Him, asking me to turn a certain direction. Even When I personally wanted to turn the other way, I obeyed and now I can see the good results.

In the depths of life's turmoil, a radiant light shine bright – the Holy Spirit. Today's main verse in another translation adds an extra word to the end of it. Do not quench the Spirit's fire. As we navigate life's unpredictable journey, the Spirit's guidance is our anchor, our comfort, and our strength. Keeping the fire within assures that we are in constant and intimate communication with the Holy Ghost.

So how would one keep the fire on? By constantly searching out the truth, meditating on the word the bread of life and by sharing what you have learned from the Spirit's revelation. Simply put, we get to be what we are created for, then we do the calling (take action). Finally, we get to experience what *Matthew 6* talks about; *the kingdom of heaven* here on earth and *everything else added into it.*

I have learned to examine every situation with caution, clinging to the good. Giving thanks at all times, trusting the Spirit's strategies to overcome adversities as they come. The Holy Spirit taught me to see opportunities where others see problems and difficulties.

James 5:16 reminds us, *the effective prayer of the righteous can accomplish much.* Our prayers are powerful weapons, shaping our destiny and the lives of those around us.

In the darkest moments, Jesus walks alongside us, leaving only His footprints in the sand. He carries us in His arms, whispering words of hope and assurance.

May our light and flaming fire inspire others to seek Jesus. May our joy be contagious, our love unconditional, and our testimony unstoppable.

LET'S PRAY TOGETHER:

Good Father, God of my ancestors. Teach me to proclaim your goodness and to be joyful and constant in prayer knowing that you are my **EL SIMCHATH GILI** my overflowing joy, my supreme joy,

Help me testify every day, Your Holy name everywhere I go. *Luke 19:40* Reminds us; *Jesus replied, I tell you, if these [people] keep silent, the stones will cry out [in praise] teach* me to not be silent, Lord.

May I understand that you do not distinguish between persons. God, you do not want anyone to perish but everyone to be saved, work through me, that I may be a bearer of your light. This I ask in the powerful name of your son Jesus. Amen!

ACTION STEPS:

Pray without ceasing, even in the darkest moments, pray in the Holy Spirit's language, ask for tongues of fire.

Give thanks in every circumstance, no matter how daunting it is. Hold fast to the good, refusing to let go of hope.

Habakkuk 3:17-18 declares, *Yet I will rejoice in the Lord; I will shout in exultation in the victorious God of my salvation!*

Decree and declare victory over your life's challenges and find inner peace, say I am prosperous in Jesus's name.

LUMINOUS DAY 27

YAHWEH
EL- EMETH

"LORD GOD OF TRUTH"

Into Your hand I commit my spirit;
You have redeemed me, O Lord, the God
of truth and faithfulness.

Psalms 31:5 (AMP)

EMBRACING TRUTH AND VICTORY

The Lord will make you the head (leader) and not the tail (follower); and you will be above only, and you will not be beneath, if you listen and pay attention to the commandments of the Lord your God, which I am commanding you today, to observe them carefully.

Deuteronomy 28:13 (AMP)

REFLECTION:

In a world where deception and falsehoods reigns, we stand firm on the unshakeable foundation of the Lord, God of Truth. Let us declare as *Psalm 31 "Into Your hand I commit my spirit; You have redeemed me, O Lord, the God of truth and faithfulness.* This powerful statement reminds us that our trust and hope are anchored in The One who is truth incarnate.

As we navigate treacherous landscapes, *Deuteronomy* reminds us; *The Lord has made you and I leaders and not followers; and to stand above and not beneath in this falling world.* We are not mere mortals; we are sons and daughters of the Sovereign King, empowered to operate under His kingdomship, power and authority. This promise is not just a distant hope but a present reality for those who trust in Jesus and are obedient to His commandments.

We are in a season where evil is called good and good is called evil, we must rise up and anchor ourselves in the *truth* of Christ Jesus in *John 14:6.* The *way* and the *life* that guides us, illuminating the path of righteousness and exposing the darkness that seeks to deceive us daily.

You and I are beyond human beings of flesh and blood. *For we are His workmanship [His own master work, a work of art], created in Christ Jesus [reborn from above—spiritually transformed, renewed, ready to be used] for good works, which God prepared [for us] beforehand [taking paths which He set], so that we would walk in them [living the good life which He prearranged and made ready for us] Eph 2:10.*

You and I face battles that are not ours but God's, so we must stand firm, armed with the sword of the Spirit, the Word of God. Unwavering, knowing whose side we are on, on this earth. You and I are in partnership with the most high.

We are not victims; we are the head, victors seated in heavenly places, with divine power. *Luke 10:19 reminds us, I have given you authority [that you now possess] to tread on serpents and scorpions, and [the ability to exercise authority] over all the power of the enemy (Satan); and nothing will [in any way] harm you.* This promise is our inheritance, we are empowered to overcome any obstacle and defeat the forces of darkness all the time.

LET'S PRAY TOGETHER:

Dear Heavenly Father, thank you for redeeming me through Jesus' precious blood. I claim my inheritance, restored with interest, as written in the Book of Life. You placed me above, as head and not the tail. Your eternal love secures me. Renew my mind, Holy Spirit, that I may grasp the mysteries of salvation. Help me learn, remember, and meditate on Your Word every day.

I choose to serve You, Lord, with my household. I want us to encounter your Glory as it says it in *Haggai 2:9 "The latter glory of this house will be greater than the former,' says the LORD OF HOSTS, 'and in this place I shall give [the ultimate] peace and prosperity,' declares the LORD OF HOSTS."* Thank you, father May Your latter glory brings us peace. Thank you for Your love and mercy, I ask in Jesus' powerful name. Amen!

ACTION STEPS:

Commit to seeking truth, wisdom and to be obedient to what God tells you to do. Stand firm in your identity as a child of God, learn how to exercise Jesus's power and authority over the enemy when he rises up against you and your loved ones.

Meditate on God's Word daily, begin your day declaring victory over all your situations, plead the blood of Jesus for your protection. Never forget you are to walk by faith and not by sight, be conscious of the spiritual realm that surrounds you. God will charge His angels to guard you.

LUMINOUS DAY 28

EMMANUEL

"GOD WITH US"

*Behold, the virgin shall become pregnant
and give birth to a Son, and they shall call His
name Emmanuel—which, when translated
means, God with us.*

Matthew. 1:23 (AMPC)

GOD'S MASTER PLAN

*For I know the plans and thoughts that
I have for you,' says the Lord, 'plans for peace and
well-being and not for disaster, to give you a
future and a hope.*

Jeremiah 29:11 (AMP)

REFLECTION:
The sovereignty of our Father is incomparable, His love endures forever. Let's read it from the message translation: *I know what I'm doing. I have it all planned out—plans to take care of you, not abandon you, plans to give you the future you hope for.* **Emmanuel** is surely with us and for us during these turbulent times we are living in.

Let us take a few moments and consider a few questions. Do we really trust God at His word? When we are going through hardship, do we truly believe He has good plans for us and not to harm us? These are genuine questions we should ask ourselves.

As we take the steps to follow and serve Jesus. Is imperative that we BELIEVE His words as they are the master key to either having a prosperous and successful life. We have a choice, do you and I want to settle to live the total opposite to the reality of a prosperous life.

Following Jesus is literally a choice of life and death. His words are *spirit and life John 6:63 living and active Heb 4:12* and if we don't believe His Intentions are good enough for us then you and I end up making decisions on our own or worse off we are guided by unseen influencers.

I'm sure you and I have lived through times where we have seen the consequences of our wrong decisions, never did we imagine the negative impact of their outcome.

Consider Peter's story in *Luke 5:4-7* Peter (Simon) and his partners worked all night and didn't catch anything yet he listened to Jesus's words. *And when he had finished speaking, he said to Simon, "Put out into the deep and let down your nets for a catch." And Simon answered, "Master, we toiled all night and took nothing! But at your word I will let down the nets." And when they had done this, they enclosed a large number of fish, and their nets were breaking. They signaled to their partners in the other boat to come and help them. And they came and filled both the boats, so that they began to sink.*

Are you ready for your net breaking miracles? I sure am!

Despite Peter's discouraging night, Jesus' word brought a miraculous catch, a life changing moment in the presence of the almighty. Don't be swayed by circumstances or negativity, learn to walk by faith.

Trust God's master plan for your life. When uncertainty and fear creep in, remember *Jeremiah 31:3, The Lord appeared to me... saying, 'I have loved you with an everlasting love; I have drawn you with unfailing kindness.*

Jesus paid the ultimate price for your freedom. Walk with confidence, knowing you're *seated in heavenly places Eph 2:6* **Emmanuel**, God with us *Matthew 1:23 will never leave nor forsake you.*

LET'S PRAY TOGETHER:
Emmanuel, Father of glory, thank you for being by my side at all times. Thank you so much for all the people that you have put in my life, help me to continue to grow in your ways. Replace my ideas with yours, renew my mind and help me see that I am a new creation in You.

Give me wisdom to be able to make the right decisions, following the divine design for which you created me. I declare that I am more than a conqueror. Thank you for choosing me and for being my Lord and Savior. All this I pray in the name that is above every name, Christ Jesus. Amen!

ACTION STEPS:

Today, make up your mind and free yourself from the lies of the enemy.

When the enemy brings thoughts of defeat and tells you that you can't do what you desire in your heart to do, tell him: *"I can do all this through him who gives me strength." Phil 4:13*

When he bombardes your mind. Do not give up, read God's word and declare it day and night. His Glory is upon you! *"You will also decide and decree a thing, and it will be established for you; And the light [of God's favor] will shine upon your ways. Job 22:28.*

Speak up the truth! *But the word is near you, in your mouth and in your heart, so that you may obey it. Dt 30:14. If you remain in me and my words remain in you, ask whatever you wish, and it will be done for you. John 15:7*

LUMINOUS DAY 29

EL CHAIYAI

"GOD OF MY LIFE"

*Yet the Lord will command His
lovingkindness in the daytime, And in the night
His song will be with me, A prayer to the God of my life.*

Psalms 42:8 (AMP)

IT'S SPIRITUAL

*God is spirit [the Source of life, yet
invisible to mankind], and those who worship Him
must worship in spirit and truth."*

John 4:24 (AMP)

REFLECTION:

Today, I invite the luminous presence of our omnipresent God to envelop us. As *John* reminds us, *God is spirit and truth*, and true worship requires surrendering to His infinite spiritual nature. This reflection will be a little different than the usual ones, I trust you will enjoy it.

Reflecting on His Omnipresence

Our God transcends space and time, existing everywhere, always. He's the essence of our existence. He is our environment as air is to the birds and water is to the fish.

For in him we live and move and exist. As some of your own poets have said, 'We are his offspring. Acts 17:28 One God and Father of all, who is over all and through all and in all. Ph 4:6 God reigns over, under, outside, within, above, and below. Guess what? You and I can too, when we begin to serve His purpose in our lives.

Freedom in the Spirit

I had a dream on March 30 2024 and in this dream, I was being silenced. I screamed and screamed the word, it's Spiritual but my children in the dream couldn't hear me nor understand and I woke up screaming. Why do I tell you this? We must know that all we see now was first in the spirit realm. Since the beginning of creation everything was formed out of God's word, He spoke and it became and in the same way you and I are created to be in His image. *We are to call things that are not as if they already are. Rom 4:17*

In Christ, you and I have freedom *2 Cor 3:17*. The Spirit within unlocks liberty, empowering us to pray, intercede, worship in spirit and truth and to do greater things. This freedom isn't bound by time or space nor matter; *Ps 139:7-10* it's a Spiritual connection with the trinity within.

Special Promises

Acts 2:1-4 and *17* Born again in Christ, His Spirit given to us, resides in us to equip us to prophesy, see visions, and dream dreams, again to do the greater things here on earth.

Become a true worshiper

Jesus said that the time had come when it no longer mattered where you worship the Father. God's point is that the *place* of worship has nothing to do with the integrity of worship, neither the style is relevant. The physical elements are not a concern. King David expressed his gratitude very well in *Ps 9:1-2*. We can come to God in every emotion and recognize His love for us individually.

Becoming a worshiper is not an outward expression or physical observance but an inward attitude that acknowledges God's greatness. We learn to honor Him as the supreme authority. You and I can become worshipers to demonstrate adoration for an audience of One, The Almighty.

May our worship be a reflection of His infinite nature, and may you and I experience the freedom and power that comes from constantly being in His presence.

LET'S PRAY TOGETHER:

God of my life, **EL CHAIYAI**. I want to express my love for you. May praises be in my mouth in spirit and truth. Let me not be ashamed when I am moved to pray in tongues, that I may recognize that you have the power over all things and to turn any situation around.

I pray that I may remain in you as your word says; *John 15:4 Remain in me, as I also remain in you. No branch can bear fruit by itself; it must remain in the vine. Neither can you bear fruit unless you remain in me.* Father, I want to be able to bear much fruit. All this I ask in the name of Yeshua HaMashiach, Jesus the messiah. Amen!

ACTION STEPS:

Recognize and acknowledge His omnipresence *Acts 17:28, Psalm 139:7-10 and* surrender to His Spirit *2 Cor 3:17*

Practice worshiping in the spirit, find a special time for intimacy with your creator, remember to express gratitude at all times.

Reflect on your thoughts and actions, ensuring alignment with God's will for your life and your loved ones.

LUMINOUS DAY 30

EL EMUNAH

"THE FAITHFUL GOD

Therefore know [without any doubt] and understand that the Lord your God, He is God, the faithful God, who is keeping His covenant and His [steadfast] lovingkindness to a thousand generations with those who love Him and keep His commandments;

Deuteronomy 7:9 (AMP)

CHOOSE LIFE

*For I have no pleasure in the death of
anyone who dies," says the Lord God.
"Therefore, repent and live!"*

Ezekiel 18:32 (AMP)

REFLECTION:

We were created for eternity. God's original intention was for us to live eternally and forever. And guess what that desire on God's heart hasn't changed. He never meant for us to expire at a certain age. No! that came about since evil kept growing and more people are falling away from His master plan.

In fact, unless that time of calamity is shortened, not a single person will survive. But it will be shortened for the sake of God's chosen ones. According to Mat 24:22

There is still time to truly return our hearts back to the Lord.

You and I were not and are not a mistake. We are a masterpiece, crafted by God's loving hands. *Genesis 1:27* reminds us, *God created man in His own image, in the image and likeness of God He created him; male and female He created them*. He knew us before we were in our mother's womb.

In Dt 30:19, God *sets before us life and death, blessings and curses*. He invites us to *choose life*. This choice reflects our God-given free will, a gift that allows us to become thinking beings, not puppets. This gift is not without controversy. *The Lord is not slow in keeping his promise, as some understand slowness. Instead he is patient with you, not wanting anyone to perish, but everyone to come to repentance. 2 Pt 3:9*

Like I mentioned at the beginning God's primary intention was eternity and He created us for it. So we would be able to take dominion over all creation, to share His divine nature and to live in communion with Him. Like a loving Father, He desires daily fellowship with His children.

His mercy endures forever, and His faithfulness is unwavering *Rom 3:3-4*. He is the same yesterday, today, and forever.

At the same time just like Abraham's example in *Gen 18:24 What if there are fifty righteous people in the city? Will you really sweep it away and not spare[a] the place for the sake of the fifty righteous people in it?* We too are called and it should inspire us to intercede for others that have fallen away.

Let's continue to recognize that we carry Christ's image *Gal 2:20* and the authority has been given to us to do so. You and I can stand in the gap for those who may be lost. We are to intercede for our government as well as our nations. It is not just about a person or a group of people but the entire world God cares about.

LET'S PRAY TOGETHER:

Father, thank You for creating me in Your image and likeness. Help me to embrace my identity and live according to Your eternal plan. Grant me wisdom to choose life and bless others through my prayers and actions.

Father of glory, my soul praises you, blessed be your holy name. Thank you for your benevolence, for always wanting the best for me. I acknowledge that you gave your son Jesus to save my life, for the forgiveness of my sins and those of the world. Thank you!

I want to forgive those who have wronged me, just as the "Our Father" in *Matthew* tells us, *"And forgive us our sins, just as we forgive those who have wronged us."* May I grasp the important meaning of this model prayer, so that I can be freed from the attacks of the evil one.

Cleanse me with your precious blood from all bitterness, discouragement, and heartbreak. Teach me to love for you are love. All this I ask in the mighty name of Jesus! Amen!

ACTION STEPS:

Set aside time for prayer, interceding for family, friends, especially for those that have being kidnapped and are being treated violently, call on God's angels to deliver them.

Study Abraham's story in *Genesis 18:24*, inspiring your own prayers.

Reflect on *Romans 3:3-4*, trusting God's unchanging love and faithfulness, share your faith with others in God's love. Journal instances where God has demonstrated His faithfulness in your life

Participate in outreach or ministry opportunities in your parish or church, serving others. Seek mentorship and or accountability for spiritual growth.

YAHWEH RAPHA

"THE LORD IS YOUR HEALER"

saying, "If you will diligently listen and pay attention to the voice of the Lord your God, and do what is right in His sight, and listen to His commandments, and keep [foremost in your thoughts and actively obey] all His precepts and statutes, then I will not put on you any of the diseases which I have put on the Egyptians; for I am the Lord who heals you."

Exodus 15:26 (AMP)

JESUS' FINISHED WORK

*"And they overcame and conquered him
because of the blood of the Lamb and because of the
word of their testimony, for they did not love their life and
renounce their faith even when faced with death."*

Revelation 12:11 (AMP)

REFLECTION:

Make this declaration today, I stand victorious, empowered by the blood of Jesus and the word of my testimony. I am a conqueror, not because of my strength, but because of Jesus' triumph over darkness.

In times of difficulty and tribulation, I often recall Jehoshaphat's story *2 Chr 20:15*. God reminds me there, that *the battle is not mine*, but His. That my faith is not in what I see, but in the One who called me into existence.

Here is another unforgettable story that often comes back to mind, this one I heard from a preacher named Jesse Duplantis, John and I went to a conference he was speaking at along with Kenneth Copeland.

A grandfather and his grandson went to the chicken coop in their backyard to find a chicken for dinner. The grandpa took the animal and put a foot on its neck and cut it off. When he removed his foot, the hen began to jump around and the child began to run. Wherever the boy ran the chicken seemed to run right behind him. In the end the little one found himself at a dead-end in the backyard, there seemed no way out.

Meanwhile, he realized that his grandpa wouldn't stop laughing. The boy asked him what he was laughing about. Grandpa replied in laughter that the chicken was dead. The scared boy replied but it's chasing after me. It's dead, he assured the boy, and he proceeded to show him the severed head.

Unfortunately, that story is a reality for many Christians today, the lack of the knowledge and truth of the authority that has been given to us here on earth, has us running even from our own shadows aimlessly, with no place to hide.

Luke 10:19 tells you and I; *Listen carefully: I have given you authority [that you now possess] to tread on serpents and scorpions, and [the ability to exercise authority] over all the power of the enemy (Satan); and nothing will [in any way] harm you.*

Jesus paid the ultimate price, His precious blood, so we can walk in freedom and to help others along the journey.

On the cross, Jesus declared, *'It is finished!' John 19:30.* And right after; *In this way, he disarmed the spiritual rulers and authorities. He shamed them publicly by his victory over them on the cross. Col 2:15*

His work is complete; now it's our turn to *diligently listen and pay attention to the voice of the Lord, and do what is right in His sight, listen to His commandments and to obey them.* We have overcome!

LET'S PRAY TOGETHER:
Lamb of God, I praise you and bless you. Lord, grant me your peace, that peace that surpasses all understanding. I ask that you cleanse and deliver me from the hands of the enemy, with your precious blood that fell from your head when they placed the crown of thorn on it.

Open my spiritual eyes so I can see from your perspective, my ears so I can hear you clearly and my mouth so I can speak your truth. I want to live by faith and not by sight, knowing that you have conquered the world.

Lord Jesus, enable me to fulfill the purpose for which I have been created, so I can be the best version of you here on earth, so that your light shines through me everywhere I go. All this I ask in Jesus Christ the Messiah. Amen!

ACTION STEPS:

Seek the Holy Spirit's guidance, study God's Word, free yourself from the enemy's tricks, John 8:36. Jesus is the only way; His name is above all names Phi 2:9-11

Meditate on Revelation 12:11 and Luke 10:19. Study the Bible, focusing on Jesus' finished work.

Challenge yourself this year to share your testimony with as many people as you can and encourage them to pray to receive Jesus in their heart.

Exercise your authority, standing against fear and doubt.

Declaration of Faith

I am victorious in Christ. The enemy has been defeated by the blood His precious. I will stand in my authority, proclaiming the gospel, and walking in freedom.

FINAL WORDS FROM THE AUTHOR

Before I was in my mother's womb, God had already chosen me to live in victory in all areas of my life. I truly believe we were all born with a divine purpose. Do not let religiosity fill your mind with uncertainties, God is able to reach out to us no matter how low we may have fallen.

I am a faithful witness of the Lord's mercy. When I saw no way out of many of my difficult situations, God had already provided a solution for them. No matter how many times I failed, God was always waiting for me to turn around to His providence to guide my steps. Many times, I thought I had no forgiveness, but God forgave me and gave me Inner Peace. His desire is to have an intimate relationship with us his children.

Below I have included some verses that have helped me in my journey with the Great I AM, which you can take, study and declare in your personal life. When it feels that you have no way out and all doors have closed around you. You can stand firmly in faith and trust that it's only a matter of time for your breakthrough. Remember when counting your blessings & victories, all glory belongs to the Almighty, His name is JESUS!

2 Corinthians 10:4-5

The weapons of our warfare are not physical [weapons of flesh and blood]. Our weapons are divinely powerful for the destruction of fortresses. We are destroying sophisticated arguments and every exalted and proud thing that sets itself up against the [true] knowledge of God, and we are taking every thought and purpose captive to the obedience of Christ,

Isaiah 54:17

"No weapon that is formed against you will succeed; And every tongue that rises against you in judgment you will condemn. This [peace, righteousness, security, and triumph over opposition] is the heritage of the servants of the Lord, and this is their vindication from Me," says the Lord.

3 John 1:2

Beloved, I pray that in every way you may succeed and prosper and be in good health [physically], just as [I know] your soul prospers [spiritually].

Romans 12:2

And do not be conformed to this world [any longer with its superficial values and customs] but be transformed and progressively changed [as you mature spiritually] by the renewing of your mind [focusing on godly values and ethical attitudes], so that you may prove [for yourselves] what the will of God is, that which is good and acceptable and perfect [in His plan and purpose for you].

Jeremiah 29:11

For I know the plans and thoughts that I have for you,' says the Lord, 'plans for peace and well-being and not for disaster, to give you a future and a hope.

Romans 6:13

Do not go on offering members of your body to sin as instruments of wickedness. But offer yourselves to God [in a decisive act] as those alive [raised] from the dead [to a new life], and your members [all of your abilities—sanctified, set apart] as instruments of righteousness [yielded] to God.

Revelation 3:7- 8

"And to the angel (divine messenger) of the church in Philadelphia write: "These are the words of the Holy One, the True One, He who has the key [to the house] of David, He who opens, and no one will [be able to] shut, and He who shuts and no one opens: 'I know your deeds. See, I have set before you an open door which no one is able to shut, for you have a little power, and have kept My word, and have not renounced or denied My name.

1 Corinthians 15:57

but thanks be to God, who gives us the victory [as conquerors] through our Lord Jesus Christ.

ABOUT THE AUTHOR

Claribel Ramírez is passionate about reading and describes herself as a very blessed woman to have an intimate and personal communion with the Holy Spirit, she loves the supernatural of God.

She is happily married to Anibal, a business entrepreneur, she is the mother of 3 Ashley 24, Jeremy 21 and John 14. Before getting married, she went through tormenting moments as a single mother and many difficult situations.

She testifies that Anibal is and was an angel sent from above to her and her children's lives when they most needed it.

Claribel loves the supernatural things of the Lord and she has carried out many missions' trips since late 2018. She now travels on a regular basis to Guatemala and Dominican Republic to spread the Gospel to the people of the nations. In April 2023 her and John traveled to Mexico to pray for the sick at a convention with the Encounter School of Ministry that she graduated from the year prior.

She and her husband Anibal have become very successful business entrepreneurs, guided by God's direction. They say that they do not take a step without first presenting it to the Lord to allow the guidance of the Holy Spirit. Claribel's greatest desire is to continue to work as a missionary and bring the good news to all the nations, as she has felt for many years in her heart and God has shown her since she was young.

You can contact her at: Jeremyjohnashley@gmail.com or write to her at Luminous Days. Visit her organization webpage GR Eternal Foundation Inc- Eternalshift.com

You can find some of her Christian videos on her YouTube channel, Instagram and TikTok, Search her full name or Clary

Ramirez. Join her and subscribe to her channel to help her grow so others can hear the good news.

https://www.youtube.com/channel/UCKpEaNmqa_Gjbad3WvOgzmg